For Lyle Sears, my colleague in the Flying Circus and pilot in the 531st — with happy memories and many best wishes for the year ahead — Hope to see you in October!

Wighm

Dec. '05

(Can you believe it has been over 60 years?)

# THE
# FLYING
# CIRCUS

# THE
# FLYING
# CIRCUS

PACIFIC WAR
—— 1943 ——
AS SEEN THROUGH A BOMBSIGHT

## JIM WRIGHT

**THE LYONS PRESS**

Guilford, Connecticut
An imprint of The Globe Pequot Press

For my five grandsons,
Chris, Erik, Kevin, Stephen, and John

––––––––––––––––

The Lyons Press is an imprint of The Globe Pequot Press.

10  8  6  4  2  1  3  5  7  9

Printed in the United States of America

Library of Congress Cataloging-in-Publication Data

Wright, Jim, 1922–
   The flying circus : Pacific war—1943—as seen through a bombsite / James C. Wright.
      p. cm.
   ISBN 1-59228-656-9 (trade cloth)
   1. Wright, Jim, 1922– 2. United States. Army Air Forces. Bomb Group (H), 380th. 3. World War, 1939–1945—Regimental histories—United States. 4. World War, 1939–1945—Aerial operations, American. 5. World War, 1939–1945—Campaigns—Pacific Area. 6. World War, 1939–1945—Personal narratives, American. 7. Bombardiers—United States—Biography. I. Title.
D790.253380th .W74 2005
940.54'4973'092—dc22

                                                                         2005002974

# CONTENTS

*If we who were there do not tell of war, the stories*
*will be left to the historians, the novelists, the mythmakers,*
*the moviemakers, the politicians—those old men*
*who send boys to kill boys like themselves.*

—DONALD M. MURRAY
*My Twice-Lived Life*

PREFACE

THIS IS A TALE ABOUT A BUNCH of fellows who made up the
380th Heavy Bomb Group in World War II, and our crowd's part in
the Pacific War. Most of these events occurred in 1943 when—except
for a tiny Allied toehold in southern New Guinea—the Japanese
occupied all the islands that encircled the northern part of Australia.

Legend has it that, in March of that year, General Eugene Eubank
came out to Lowry Field in Denver to inspect the 380th before we
went overseas. Our flying and marching formations were so sloppy,
as the story goes, that he exclaimed, "My God, it's a flying circus!"

Our commanding officer, a lieutenant colonel named William
A. Miller, instead of cringing from the general's pejorative charac-
terization, had the wit to embrace it. The appellation was, to say the
least, distinctive. Thereafter, Col. Miller wore that name as a badge
of honor, and it stuck.

This is a strictly limited take on the whole thing, as seen by a second lieutenant from Weatherford, Texas, a bombardier who spent

the twenty-first year of his life with this aggregation and lived, by the grace of God, to tell about it a long time later.

That's me. I'm Jim Wright, and a whole lot older now. The trouble is, I didn't begin to write all this down until 2001, which was about fifty-eight years late. And I wasn't anywhere close to the guys who actually ran the show in those days and could have provided more strategic insights. There was a lot I didn't know, and I've undoubtedly forgotten a lot of what I did.

But war can be an intensely personal matter, after all, and some things you don't forget. That's the war I want to tell you about.

Why did I decide, after all these years, to write this memoir? It began as a letter to my grandchildren. A prominent Fort Worth citizen named Val Willkie, in the spring of 2001, sent me and several other friends a fascinating story from his own World War II experience. He'd written it, he said, for his grandchildren. Val challenged us to do the same.

But Willkie's tale awakened even broader pangs of conscience. None of us who'd known Val casually for many years knew he'd flown a B-17 in Europe, let alone that he was shot down over Holland, sought sanctuary in Dutch farm homes, was helped by the underground, and almost escaped before being captured by the Nazis to spend a year as their prisoner of war.

Like most of us who fought in that war, Willkie had clammed up for decades behind an unspoken code of silence. It just wasn't considered good form in our day to talk about wartime experiences. They were something we wanted to put behind us. Realizing now that a chapter of unwritten history is closing with each funeral of a contemporary, several of us vowed to write down what authentic stories we could remember.

Just then, I received an appeal from Stephen Ambrose. That celebrated chronicler of so many valuable memories of World War II, mostly with a European focus, was asking some of us who'd fought in the Pacific to record personal anecdotes of that time and place, lest they be forgotten forever. It is sad that Ambrose died before he could collate these personal tales of the Pacific War into one grand piece.

Then came September 11. The numbing surprise of the terrorist atrocities at the World Trade Center and the Pentagon evoked nationwide recollections of that day at Pearl Harbor, sixty years before. People everywhere began comparing America's current situation with that we faced in World War II. Then, in late spring, 2004, public response to the dedication of the World War II Memorial in Washington and the sixtieth anniversary observance of D-Day revealed a great and growing hunger to capture and preserve all the floating memories of that wonderful, terrible, magical time we called World War II.

Each new development seemed to give new urgency to my task that began, so simply, as a letter to my five grandsons. And the more I wrote, the more I remembered. Along with the similarities of our two times, there also were significant, gaping differences.

It is tempting to people my age to luxuriate mentally in Tom Brokaw's generous assessment of our generational character. "The Greatest Generation" asserts an extravagant claim. But in our heart of hearts we know that we were not extraordinary people, just fairly malleable young folks, products of our times and of our parents' guidance. Hitler once described us as "decadent." He considered Americans indolent and soft. We weren't that, either.

Donald Murray in his memoir, *My Twice-Lived Life*, opines that surviving the Great Depression had inoculated us against despair and toughened our capacity for hard challenges. "Through it all, our unexpected survival has made most of us optimists," he writes, "quietly, even secretly, confident about our individual ability to cope."

If, in our zeal to improve life for our progeny, we'd somehow failed to pass on to them that ability to cope with the unexpected, it occurs to me that we haven't been so great at all. Our parents, I believe, passed it on to us as we watched them make do with little.

The fellowship of sacrifice developed during the Great Depression and World War II built a sense of national camaraderie that Americans haven't known before or since. May God forbid that we shall need it again for our survival. But if we do, I pray and believe that it lies there still, dormant in the national psyche. If it doesn't, our generation really didn't do so well, after all, by those we raised.

My grandchildren's contemporaries are bigger, smarter, healthier, and more highly educated than we were. I have faith they are as patriotic and unselfish when need arises. Anyhow, this is a story of the way *we* were, *then*.

And the place to begin is in recognizing, at the outset, just how this war was, indeed, a very different war from any other we've experienced.

—JIM WRIGHT
FORT WORTH, TEXAS

# I

## A VERY DIFFERENT WAR

"YESTERDAY, DECEMBER SEVENTH, 1941—a date which will live in infamy . . ." The vibrant baritone of President Franklin Delano Roosevelt intoned the words, unhurriedly caressing every syllable of what arguably would be his most unforgettable line in that long career of memorable lines and persuasive oratory.

A dwindling number of us can also still recall to memory's ear the sound of resonant Rooseveltian confidence transmitted in his first inaugural address almost nine years earlier: "The only thing we have to fear is fear itself." I was ten then. But those words still fit our situation in 1941.

On that Monday morning of December 8, Roosevelt had reviewed and polished the phrases of the brief speech to Congress asking for a declaration of war. At the last minute he took a fountain pen from his inner coat pocket and scratched out the final word in the opening clause of the prepared text. FDR drew a line through the original word, *history*, and in his handwritten cursive substituted *infamy*. The word was his. Though unfamiliar to many Americans, its meaning was universally felt.

Almost every American who'd attained the age of, say, ten (and many younger) could tell people exactly where and in what circumstances they had first heard the galvanizing news of the Japanese attack on Pearl Harbor. Most of us still living nearly sixty years later, on September 11, 2001, reflexively recalled the timeless mental imagery of December 7, 1941. As we stared in disbelieving horror at repeated television news depictions of that hijacked airliner crashing head-on into the World Trade Center tower, our minds sprang involuntarily back to Pearl Harbor.

There was no television, of course, in 1941, with its unrivaled power to hold a nation transfixed. We had to depend on radio to shock and inform us. To alarm, and outrage us. And ultimately to unite us. What the sneak strike by the assault aircraft of the imperial Japanese armada had done to our fleet lying at anchor in Pearl Harbor, Hawaii, and to thousands of unsuspecting innocents was, for us, every bit as horrifying as the televised images of 9/11 would be to our children's and grandchildren's generations, six decades later.

Aside from that shared sense of national outrage evoked by those two spectacular events, there were, of course, significant differences in the two occasions. World War II differs in important ways from any other conflict in America's history. For one thing, that war was, literally, forced upon us. We had no option but to fight. Nor has any other conflict since the Civil War so directly and vitally threatened our national survival. Nor has another demanded of the American people such nearly universal sacrifice and cooperation. Nor has any other conflict aroused such an overpowering national sense of both unity and urgency.

By the morning of December 8, we knew exactly who the enemy was. They'd made no effort to conceal their identity, or their intention to destroy us. Hence we knew exactly what we had to do. An unprovoked act of war had been committed against the nation— killing more than 2,300 of our countrymen, sinking the battleship *Arizona* and capsizing the *Oklahoma*, as well as other ships in the harbor, destroying 180 American airplanes, and wreaking havoc with numerous other craft, docks, and facilities, both military and civilian. All in one day's work, though secretly planned for months.

We were at war, declaration or not. Within days, both the other Axis powers, Nazi Germany and Fascist Italy, had declared war on us. It would be a fight to the finish, no holds barred. Total war. A long, hard, and costly fight for our national survival.

To recapture the spirit that pervaded wartime America, it is necessary to go back and briefly revisit a few of the events that preceded and laid preface to December 7, 1941.

FOR MONTHS THE UNITED STATES HAD BEEN in the process of being drawn inexorably into the vortex of a spreading worldwide conflagration. Actually, the process had begun ten years earlier, on September 18, 1931, when the Japanese army marched lawlessly into Manchuria, setting up a global chain of events that would have their climax at Pearl Harbor. Japan's unannounced and unchecked invasion of China encouraged others to embark upon similar trails of marauding military expansionism. Mussolini, empire-hungry, stormed into Ethiopia in 1935; Hitler's troops occupied the legally demilitarized Rhineland, then invaded the Sudetenland, then Czechoslovakia, Austria, and finally in 1939, Poland, which drew England and France into the struggle to resist Germany's worldwide ambitions. Undeterred, Hitler invaded Russia.

Meanwhile, the disciplined Japanese warlords subdued not only Manchuria but more of China, and by 1941 had seized control of all Indochina. Now, they viewed our country as the only remaining impediment to fulfilling their thirst to rule Asia and all the Pacific. Geographically confined for centuries on their tight, overcrowded little islands, they long had coveted the Pacific's sprawling treasure-house of raw materials—oil, tin, copper, rubber—to feed and fuel Japan's surging military and industrial ambitions. For them, now, there was no turning back. These were the realities that December, the fruits of a decade of unarrested military aggression.

Some Americans had seen the dimensions of the rising threat and the near inevitability of its denouement. In 1940, France fell before the advancing Nazi juggernaut. President Roosevelt was at first barred by the Neutrality Act from offering any tangible assistance to Great Britain, which now stood alone, save for the embattled Soviet Union, in resistance to Hitler's bloody and seemingly insatiable territorial ambitions.

NOBODY DOUBTED, HOWEVER, where the American president's sympathies, and those of most Americans, lay.

After the elections of 1940, Mr. Roosevelt having been awarded an historically unprecedented third term, he strove for national unity. He appointed two well-known Republicans to his cabinet. One was Henry L. Stinson, President Herbert Hoover's Secretary of State, whom FDR made Secretary of War (a moral equivalent of our modern Secretary of Defense). Then, in a broad gesture of bipartisanship, FDR asked his recently defeated Republican presidential opponent, Wendell Willkie, to serve as his personal emissary to Prime Minister Winston Churchill.

Roosevelt handed Willkie a copy of Longfellow's poem to carry personally to the embattled prime minister:

> . . . Sail on, O Ship of State!
> Sail on, O Union, strong and great!
> Humanity with all its fears,
> With all the hopes of future years,
> Is hanging breathless on thy fate!

To this, our president appended a personal, handwritten note saying that those words applied to the British people at that moment, as well as to Americans.

The grisly old wordsmith, Churchill, replied publicly to FDR in a BBC broadcast, carried live by shortwave to the United States. His was an emotional utterance of thanks, ending with the unashamed plea: "Give us the tools, and we'll finish the job."

Finally, Roosevelt created an innovative way around the legalistic prohibitions of the Neutrality Act by persuading Congress to approve the Lend-Lease Bill. The artful premise was that we weren't *giving* these planes and tanks and other implements of war to England, but merely *lending* and/or *leasing* them to our British cousins—and later, by extension, to the Soviet Union. If this could be called disingenuous, it was—most agreed—ingenious.

THERE WERE ISOLATIONISTS and wishful thinkers who hoped we could somehow dodge involvement. And a few naive idealists who didn't understand the nature of the Axis leadership mentality. They cheerfully believed in peace and in setting examples of peace. A lot of folks in the late '30s simply had no comprehension of how ill prepared we were militarily and how long it would take to mobilize and train a fighting force if and when the war were brought to us. During my first two years in college I was one of those.

When Congress voted in 1940 to impose America's first peacetime draft, I was the newly designated editor of the Weatherford College newspaper.

There were only about three hundred students at the small, two-year Methodist institution, but my assistant editor Harold Owen and I had contrived to print about two thousand extra copies of each eight-page edition for free distribution throughout the community. This, among other things, permitted us to increase the advertising rate from fifty cents to sixty cents a column inch. It cost thirty dollars to run off each edition at a local print shop. By arrangement with college officialdom, anything we earned above this amount in advertising we sold, my assistant Harold Owen and I split between us.

In the two issues prior to the vote in Congress, I wrote flaming editorials, denouncing the draft as dictatorial, militaristic, and un-American. It was also, I wrote, an insult to the patriotism of American youth. If our country were ever threatened, I vowed, we wouldn't need to be drafted but would beat such a path to volunteer our services that we'd wear out the front steps of the nation's recruiting offices!

Powerful stuff! Yet how foolish. How insufferably self-righteous. I'd thank God later that wiser judgment had prevailed, when I contemplated how infinitely more difficult would have been our national task in 1942 were it not for that large corps of trained and disciplined people whipped into shape by a year-and-a-half's head start.

Yet when that one-year draft authorization came up for renewal in mid-1941, its continuance was bitterly contested in Congress. It passed the House by precisely a one-vote margin. That late. Roughly six months before Pearl Harbor.

IN LATE SPRING OF 1941, following the death of U.S. Senator Morris Sheppard, a special election was called in Texas to replace him. Thirteen candidates announced. It was the first time I'd heard Lyndon Johnson speak. He was a thirty-two-year-old congressman running to fill the Senate vacancy. Some of my friends had been able to stay in college because of the National Youth Administration jobs they'd found when Johnson was head of that New Deal agency. Several of them were helping in his campaign, and they asked me to come with them to hear Lyndon.

The best punch line in Johnson's speech came as he discussed the explosive world situation. If the day should ever come when he as a member of Congress would have to vote to send American boys to fight and die in a foreign war, he dramatically pledged, " . . . then, on that day, will Lyndon Johnson leave his seat in the United States Senate and go with them!"

Two friends, Joe Kilgore and Sydney Reagan, had stationed themselves on opposite sides of the crowd. As soon as Lyndon's voice delivered that last ringing phrase, each of my buddies let out a loud, jubilant war whoop, and the crowd soon stampeded into a thunderous ovation.

Johnson didn't win that race. W. Lee O'Daniel did. But serving in the House just about six months or so later, on December 8, Lyndon Johnson did vote for the declaration of war—as did every other senator and representative, with only one exception: Jeanette Rankin of Montana was the lone holdout. To Johnson's credit, he kept his word, becoming the very first member in either house of Congress to leave the Capitol and enter military service. A number of others soon followed suit.

Like thousands of young men my age, I left my third-year studies at the University of Texas, where I'd been studying since the previous summer, and volunteered for service. Before the month was out I was, by my own choice, in uniform, sworn in on December 31, 1941. It wasn't that I questioned America's ability to triumph, regardless. More, I think, that I didn't want it done without my help. I wanted to be part of it. A lot of us felt that way.

Six months earlier, in the summer of 1941, three of my college classmates had left to join the Royal Canadian Air Force, so eager were they to get involved. And two others had hitched a ride with me to Fort Worth to volunteer in the Army Air Corps. It was the branch of service most favored by my crowd. Several of my friends were quick to enlist in the Air Corps and thus get their choice of service branches. Had they waited around until drafted, they'd have had to depend on the luck of the draw.

THE AMERICAN PEOPLE WERE READY—I hesitate to say anxious—to sacrifice after December 7. And it wasn't just buying a war bond and planting a Victory garden, we discovered. The total mobilization we supported, in fact demanded, involved inconveniences that permeated the daily lives of civilians. It wasn't only army and navy but a whole nation that went to war. That's an important thing to understand.

Mobilization of American industry took entire segments of ordinary commerce wholly out of production for civilian markets. No American automobile was built, save military jeeps and trucks, from the end of 1941 until it was time for 1946 models. Household appliances—refrigerators, washing machines, and the like—were frozen out of production. Factories that made them converted to producing machine-gun turrets and other commodities essential to the war.

*Use it up; wear it out; make it do; and do without*—that was the slogan, the civilian reality. Gasoline was tightly rationed. Only cars provably devoted to an essential wartime activity entitled their owners to ration coupons. Part of our national resolve was expressed in the question, "Is this trip really necessary?"

Meat, sugar, butter, and other grocery staples grew scarce on civilian tables, as America strained to make certain that men in uniform would be fed. That's when Spam and margarine became commonplace, along with meat substitutes made of soybeans. Every week had designated Meatless Days.

So it was with clothing, the need so great for uniforms. Silk stockings went off the shelves, as parachutes demanded all the silk. Leather goods were scarce. When I became an officer just less than a year after enlisting and had to buy my own dress uniform, my war-bride wife used one of her own shoe stamps to buy me a pair of dressy jodhpurs. Luxury taxes were imposed on all sorts of "optional" things like new billfolds, purses, and women's makeup.

There were price and rent controls to protect the public from price gouging on all sorts of scarce commodities. Hoarding or profiteering from scarcities brought not only government sanctions but frowns and social ostracism from one's neighbors. Young kids proudly did their bit by going around the neighborhoods gathering up scrap metal, waste, and junk for recycling.

SOME CURBS WERE PLACED on personal liberties, but probably fewer than in any other democracy at a time of total war. There was censorship of military mail, of course, to avoid any inadvertent disclosure of troop movements that could be of benefit to an enemy. But soldiers, sailors, and airmen all enjoyed free mailing. Just signing our envelopes was sufficient for postage and made us feel as important as congressmen. *Loose Lips Sink Ships* embedded itself into our minds. If you lived anywhere near the coast, you pulled the blinds at night to darken the house. The blackout, probably less severe than in Britain, engaged civilian wardens who went around the neighborhoods checking against exterior leaks in lumination.

The only real infringement upon constitutional rights, I think, was the internment of 120,000 Americans for no other reason than their Japanese ancestry, in scattered camps resembling prisoner of war habitations. This abject denial of fundamental rights was, I think, a product of early-war hysteria.

The Supreme Court in 1944 upheld that act as constitutional in time of total war, but I have to believe the justices knew better. Particularly egregious did it become to a nation whose most decorated combat unit would be the 442nd Regimental Combat Team, composed exclusively of Japanese-descended American volunteers. They fought their way to glory through heavy casualties in Italy while rescuing a surrounded National Guard contingent from Texas.

THE SPIRIT OF VOLUNTEERISM extended far beyond the likes of us healthy young guys who left school to do battle. Rosie the Riveter became a model of heroism for women throughout our land who entered factory lines, airplane cockpits, and the uniformed services for the first time in American history, to fill war-essential jobs and free men for combat.

Why, a few have asked, did I want to be a bombardier? After all, I'd learned to fly a plane. Why not a pilot? The answer probably reveals the immaturity of my rationale. But, then, we all were immature—and desperately afraid someone might notice it.

First, I was in an enormous hurry to get into combat. Foolishly, I feared the war could be over before I got involved. On my first day at camp, I formally applied for aviation cadet training. It took more than five months before I could be certified for the entrance exam, and meanwhile, I'd been promoted to corporal. Bombardier training lasted only five months; pilots required nine months. And I was in a hurry.

The second reason had to do with my unconscious, banal comparison of war with sports. My two big sports had been boxing and football. A fighter pilot I compared with a boxer—doing his thing all by himself out there in the Wild Blue arena. The teamwork of football I'd found more appealing, and associated it with the work of a bomb crew. I mentally equated the bombardier with the forward passer who throws the ball for the touchdown score.

To qualify for one's wings and second lieutenant commission at nineteen wasn't unprecedented in 1942. Nor was I unique in supposing that a second lieutenant's $225 a month, counting flying pay, might be enough to support a wife—especially if we'd already been somewhat engaged for over a year. Of course, we agreed, we'd have to do without certain luxuries and work together for the long pull. But wasn't that just what the whole country was doing?

# 2

## HURRY UP AND WAIT

ON NEW YEAR'S EVE, along with twenty-five or thirty other young North Texans, I took the oath of military service at the army recruiting facility in Dallas. We'd been billeted at the Army's expense in a small nearby hotel the night before, and had begun to get acquainted. Most, like me, were from small towns—Mount Pleasant, Red Oak, Ferris, Plano, Stephenville, Strawn. Far as I could learn, there were only two others beside myself who wanted to qualify for aviation cadet training. One of those was Garth Wade of Ferris, who'd played in the backfield for Trinity University, then located in Waxahachie, during the semester just ending. He and I would become friends.

On the night of December 30, five of us had gone out to have dinner together, redeeming meal chits we'd been issued by the recruiters. A guy from Stephenville quipped that he'd call them "chow chits" except that it sounded too much like "cow chips." The rest of us laughed because there wasn't anything else to do.

After eating, two of the five said they'd like to see *Sergeant York*, the Gary Cooper portrayal of the World War I hero, then showing at a second-run theater nearby. I knew where the movie house was and said I'd go with them. The other two didn't want to see a show, but one of them said they knew a fine whorehouse just a couple of blocks over. Having previously lived in Dallas, I had an idle curiosity to know what house he could have in mind that close to the center of downtown. The theatergoers, as it turned out, were also curious, but still wanted to see the movie, as did I. Since it was still early, we all walked along together, out of a combination of curiosity and the desire to be good sports. Nobody wanted to seem prudish.

It grew slightly embarrassing as we arrived at the front porch of the large house. Sensing our reticence, one of the Stephenville duo said, "Aw, come on in and see what it looks like inside." Curiosity and a rising sense of adventure prevailed. The first thing I noticed on entering was a fairly heavy scent of perfume. And something else I couldn't exactly define. A faint hint of incense? When time came for the two patrons to retire with partners into separate rooms down the hall somewhere, we three said we'd better go so we wouldn't miss the start of the movie. We even complimented the woman we took to be the madam on how nice the furniture looked. Seemed like a polite thing to say—especially since we weren't spending any money there. Finally, feeling increasingly foolish, we went on to the show, and afterwards back to the hotel. Our two more adventuresome colleagues found their own way home.

On New Year's Day, newly decked out in uniform and freshly shorn of almost all our hair, like summer sheep, we were given all-day passes to celebrate the holiday. By prior arrangement, I was to meet my family that noontime at the Cotton Bowl.

THE ANNUAL COTTON BOWL football classic had become a tradition for Dad and me, except for the year before when the family had spent the holiday season in California, visiting relatives. While there, Dad and I, along with assorted cousins, had seen the Rose Bowl game.

Always before in our family, however, the gridiron contest had been a male bastion. Mother and my two sisters—Mary Nelle, thirteen, and Betty Lee, eleven—were coming this year, just to see me off. Nobody could guess how long it would be before we'd be reunited.

I had made up a little speech of assurance to make the folks feel better, but as we sat there in the stands, Mother's eyes kept watering up behind her glasses. She was trying desperately not to show it, and I was pretending not to notice. When it came to an appropriate time for my inspiring comments, I got to worrying about their possible effect on Mother—maybe it would make her break down and weep publicly—and then wondered about my ability to bring it all off with anything approaching aplomb. Dad clapped me strongly on the shoulder, and the girls were staring admiringly at my army uniform, even though I was just a private and had no stripes, and there was a lump in my throat about the size of a baseball, and I honestly don't know what I said, but we each of us knew, or thought we knew, what the others were thinking.

My sisters were probably feeling proud of their older brother, thinking how heroic this all was. Maybe they thought me brave. Mother was thinking I was too young to be going away so soon, maybe remembering when she and Dad were newlyweds and he went off to France in World War I, maybe thinking of things I did when I was a little kid. Dad—well, he'd thought of several funny things to say to break the tension. He'd taught me the importance of honor, and, for example, how to smile in the face of adversity, even danger. He may have been hoping there wasn't some lesson he'd left untaught. And I? Well, I knew how fortunate I'd always been to have them. I had confidence I'd be coming back. God, how I loved them! And how I ached at that moment to have the war over and done.

THAT NIGHT OUR GROUP of new recruits was bused to Camp Wolters, near Mineral Wells, and just fifteen miles west of our home in Weatherford. We'd be there less than a week before transferring to Sheppard Field at Wichita Falls, a hundred miles or so northwest. It had been long enough for me to apply formally for flight school. I supposed, foolishly, that I'd get word of my acceptance in a week or ten days.

At Wolters, we began our series of immunization shots and were exposed to the first—some say the worst—of the Army's famous indoctrination films. This one was devised as a shock treatment to scare successive bunches of hormonal males out of their hides about the horrific lurking dangers of venereal disease.

As we piled off the buses at Sheppard, we were greeted by the taunt that every batch of new dogfaces must have heard chanted by only slightly more experienced ones since the Revolutionary War. "You'll be s-o-r-r-eey!" The last word is dragged out like the refrain of a funeral dirge.

Sheppard was boot camp. Three weeks of it, as I recall. It seemed like months. We marched everywhere we went, often at double-time, and took batteries of tests designed, I suppose, to measure our knowledge and aptitudes. The theory was, I think, to make rounder pegs out of us so they could put us in squarer holes.

Much has been made of the horrors of army food. Mostly, I think that's a bum rap. I liked the grub. Maybe I was atypical, but I think not. Most parents in those days, like mine, made a virtue of cleaning your plate. We were admonished that it was a sin to waste good food. "Think of all those starving Armenians—or hungry little Chinese children—or—." I even liked the creamed chipped beef on toast, in spite of the name it went by in the Army.

A sign in the mess hall at Sheppard proclaimed TAKE ALL YOU WANT, BUT EAT ALL YOU TAKE! I liked that sentiment. There were a few finicky fellows with effete appetites who gagged on some of the mess hall's cuisine, but they'd be excoriated by the KPs (Kitchen Police) if there was much uneaten food left on their trays when they filed past the waste bins. One told me he learned always to take a box of cereal, and if there was anything on his plate he just couldn't stomach, he'd simply stuff it, uneaten, in the empty cereal box and smile sweetly at the KP as he dumped his concealed leavings in the garbage.

We did lots of calisthenics at boot camp. One guy said even his muscles were getting muscles. Push-ups and sit-ups and knee-bends and running. The drill sergeants were hammering us into shape. And I, who'd never really made my bed, was learning how to make up a tight, neat, four-cornered bed so taut that if you flipped a quarter on it, the coin would bounce back up with the verve of a human body rebounding from a trampoline. More tests and more shots and more interviews and more close-order drill with rifles. I still hadn't heard anything about the status of my flight school application.

And I couldn't figure out how all this other stuff was going to help us win World War II.

Finally, we seemed to graduate without ceremony from boot camp, and our whole contingent was put on a troop train and shipped en masse to March Field at Riverside, California. Here, I got my first in-person look at Bob Hope, as he and a group of troupers from Hollywood or wherever put on a first-class show for our crowd of willing rubes who'd signed up from city streets and grassroots villages, farm rows and factory lines, schoolrooms and pool halls, think tanks and coal mines—all to defend our common country.

At March Field, there were more immunization shots, and I began to observe a fascinating phenomenon. You could count on it. Set your watch by it. You could be in a line of a hundred airmen, each following another in succession past a needle-bearing medic who'd administer, to each in turn, an inoculation. There'd be no problem. There wasn't supposed to be. Each would walk away, rubbing his shoulder gently.

Then, one day, some fellow would react aberrantly. He'd take his shot, suddenly lose consciousness, eyelids fluttering, his spine and knees passively collapsing, and slump down in a wad on the floor. Was the needle blunter, the chemical mix stronger, the systemic shock greater? Maybe, but I doubt it. Now, here's what's predictable: Whenever one passes out, three or four others in the waiting line, observing his plight, would lose consciousness and fall senseless when it came their turn to take the needle—some even before it hit them. I attributed it to the power of suggestion. There had to be some moral lesson from this, I thought, but never figured out exactly what it was.

AFTER A COUPLE OF WEEKS at March Field, a goodly number of us were moved to Hamilton Field, north of San Francisco, and assigned to the 14th Fighter Group. This was a very nearly combat-ready outfit, having flown P-39s and P-40s, some now transitioning into P-38s.

This, we discovered quickly, was more like what we thought the real war might resemble. Previously we were just recruits of amorphous utility. We'd had no specific responsibility of direct relevance to winning the war. Each of us now found himself being integrated into a war-bound unit, receiving an individual work assignment in the 14th Group. Now, we also began to see a semblance of reason in the lengthy interviews and batteries of tests to which we'd been subjected for the better part of six weeks.

Our barracks of assorted recruits was a heterogeneous garden of modest skills: One colleague, who'd been a short-order cook, was assigned to duty under the mess sergeant. Another, who'd worked between college semesters at a local garage, wound up in the motor pool. Because of my college editorship, maybe, or because I'd covered football games as a stringer for the *Fort Worth Star-Telegram*, or perhaps because I'd made pocket money while at the University of Texas by creating a card file system of cases and legal opinions for the Texas Attorney General's office—whatever the rationale, I found myself assigned to Group Headquarters and ordered to report to the group intelligence officer, a Captain Ayres.

The work of the Intelligence (or G-2) section held a certain fascination, and I plunged in happily, glad to have something more apparently purposeful than "squad's right" or "mark time." I soon was awarded Secret Clearance and given custody over the entire library of classified material in group possession.

These documents were kept in a big fireproof safe in the Head-quarters' Building, and I was made privy to the lock combination that opened the safe. One of my jobs was to make a cross-referenced card file system, by subject matter, making it easier to summon up information contained in each document. It dawned on me why I had probably been given this assignment. I wrote proudly to Texas Attorney General Gerald Mann and told him how I was using the skills I'd learned in his office to help the war effort. I read vora-ciously, fascinated by the material. I'd still heard nothing in reference to my application for flying officer school.

IN THOSE FIRST MONTHS, the war was not going well at all. On January 11, the Japanese invaded New Guinea and began consoli-dating territory, driving the thin line of defenders back. On the 31st their troops stormed into Manila, forcing General MacArthur's de-fending units to cede the Philippine capital and fall back, regroup-ing in outlying locations.

On February 15, following two weeks of siege, Singapore fell as outnumbered British troops surrendered that supposedly impreg-nable fortress. Two weeks later, Japanese forces, sweeping all resist-ance before them, landed on Sumatra, in the Southwest Pacific, and then on the neighboring island of Java, where they captured 100,000 Allied troops.

In Washington, President Roosevelt sent Congress his first wartime budget request. It was bold and austere. The president called for total expenditures of $59 billion for the year, the most our government had ever contemplated spending. All but $7 billion would be earmarked for the war effort. We'd have to curtail all do-mestic expenditures ruthlessly, "for the duration"—a phrase that would resonate for the next three years throughout the public dia-logue. Until the war was won, we'd put in abeyance construction of domestic highways and roads, schools, post offices, and federal buildings of all kinds.

In March, Mr. Roosevelt asked the nation's governors and legislators to reduce the top speed limit to forty miles an hour. The purpose was to save automobile tires. All the rubber we could get our hands on would be needed for military vehicles. Our rubber sources were being shut off by increasingly pervasive Japanese hegemony in the Pacific. Also, the president requested that the Congress approve $9 billion more in new taxes.

MacArthur left the Philippines in March, on presidential orders, to take up command of the united Allied forces in the Pacific. Headquarters would be in Australia. In the general's dramatic departure, he'd publicly vowed with his trademark flair, "I shall return!" All the GIs I knew winced. We thought he ought to have said, "*We* shall return!" Nonetheless, everyone recognized the contingencies of the unhappy moment. We needed some heroics. There just wasn't any good news.

Left behind to hold off, harass, and delay the inevitable Japanese consolidation of the Philippines, were General Jonathan Wainwright and a hardy force of some 36,000 Americans and Filipinos. After a savagely fought delaying action for four months on the Bataan peninsula, they ran completely out of food. They'd been on half rations for more than a month, dividing these short supplies with Filipino compatriots. Finally, on April 9, sick and famished, the game garrison fell before an onslaught of 200,000 Japanese assault troops. Most of the 36,000 were killed or captured. Wainwright escaped with a small, beleaguered remnant and began their long, harried journey that became known as the Bataan Death March.

IT WAS NOT UNTIL APRIL 18 that good-news-hungry Americans would get something to cheer about. Our spirits vaulted when a group of B-25 crews under the command of Lieutenant Colonel James H. (Jimmy) Doolittle, stealthily ensconced aboard the aircraft carrier, the USS *Hornet*, took off from a secret location in the North Sea and, six hundred miles later, surprised the world by bombing and strafing Tokyo. Moving under the protection of Admiral William Halsey's task force, the bomber-laden carrier with the B-25s concealed from view, penetrated the Japanese defense perimeter to bring sixteen camouflaged B-25s close enough for the stunning mission.

All of Japan—as well as everyone else except President Roosevelt and a few silent collaborators—was totally surprised. The sixteen medium bombers dropped their explosive payload on the complacent city, and several unsuspecting targets, and all but two crews made their getaway to a predetermined landing strip in China. "We flew in so low," Doolittle joked afterwards, "that we almost stopped to watch a ball game in progress below us." Pressed for details as to where the flyers had found a place to take off within range of Tokyo, and bomb the city without being intercepted, President Roosevelt answered, "Shangri-La." His whimsical reference was to that imaginary never-never land of idyllic peace and joy in the Himalayan Mountains, enshrined by James Hilton in his best-selling novel, *Lost Horizon.*

The bombs set fires and did some other physical damage, but this mission's purpose was less strategic than psychological. In that arena, it was our first home run! Jimmy Doolittle's name became a household word, and Americans reveled in one first, tentative but triumphal taste of success.

The Japanese military elite, meanwhile, took the raid as a grave personal insult. Their failure to protect the homeland and the city of their emperor humiliated and enraged them. They had lost *face,* that commodity of such infinite value in their military officers' caste and culture. Their overreaction took the form of an erratic reign of terror.

Concluding that Doolittle's raiders had been assisted by villagers in China, Japanese military leaders determined to visit the full weight of their wrath upon the Chinese. They quickly launched six hundred air raids, according to intelligence sources, upon towns and villages of China. Then, identifying communities through which they believed American airmen had escaped, they burned entire towns to the ground. Japanese troops—100,000 of them—turned these areas into scorched earth, shooting and bayoneting civilians indiscriminately, raping women, even strangling and drowning Chinese children. This shocking information added a new dimension to our crystallizing recognition of the complex turn of mind that some of us would soon enough confront physically.

AFTER FOUR MONTHS in the Army, I had settled into the routine. In my first month, private's pay was twenty-one dollars monthly. There was a popular song, *Twenty-one dollars-a-day, once a month!* After that, Congress raised it to thirty dollars. Something came out for "squadron fund," but that left $25 or so, and food, clothing, and shelter were on the house. After the requisite three months in grade, I was promoted to corporal. The work in the Intelligence Office was interesting. I had read and learned a lot. After hours, I'd box or play handball in the base gymnasium or kick a football with Garth Wade for thirty minutes or so every day. Army chow agreed with me, and I was getting plenty of sleep. I weighed 183, sixteen pounds more than when I'd enlisted. It was all solid. My army jacket was size forty, and my trousers were thirty inches in the waist.

But it wasn't exactly what I'd signed on for. One day someone told me a "big B-24" had landed on the base runway. I'd never seen one, but knew some of them were being built in Fort Worth. I walked over to the runway and took a long, appraising look at it. Not sleek and sexy like a B-17, but it looked solid. It had a firm, squared-off look to the fuselage, accentuated by the twin horizontal stabilizers, or tails. Why some had taken to calling this plane a "Flying Boxcar" was quickly apparent! I approved.

I learned, however, not to stand or walk behind it when the engines were revving up. A hot blast of unexpected force hit me, stinging my skin, showering me with sand and debris kicked up off the runway surface. It made me appreciate how the wall of a sandblasted building must feel!

The next morning, Group Headquarters got a disturbing call. I never knew the source. Captain Ayres asked me and a staff sergeant named Ronnie McEwen to pick up a jeep and drive with him to check out an accidental crash on a mountainside about twenty miles west of the base. "A B-24 cracked up out there a short while ago," the captain said, "and it's on fire." Could it be the same aircraft I'd visually inspected the night before, I wondered?

When we got there, the sight was sickening. The plane's fuselage seemed totally consumed, black from the carbon of the fire's toxic smoke. An acrid, dark cloud idled off, overhead and to the east. There was a noxious smell, like burning rubber. The medics were there with stretchers. McEwen and I watched as they went directly by us, each stretcher carrying a burned cadaver. Burned crisp, blackened flesh covering lifeless bodies with trickles of red blood oozing out of little crevices here and there. The relentless eye of memory brings the scene clearly back to me today. I feel again the horrifying reality: just short hours earlier, these were people—guys like me.

Spasms made me shiver and I suppressed an impulse to vomit.

Sgt. McEwen had been trying for several weeks, off and on, to talk me out of flying school. Captain Ayres, while supportive of my primary ambition, had offered—if aviation cadets didn't pan out—to recommend me for OCS. That would have been just a three-month stint, and I could continue working in the intelligence field if I chose.

Now, as the next stretcher passed us, Ronnie McEwen asked, "Do you still want to fight this war in an airplane?"

I didn't answer right away. I swallowed hard. I felt a little dizzy. When my head cleared, I said, "Yeah. Yeah, I do."

# 3

## THREE TO MAKE READY

IT WAS JUNE BEFORE I RECEIVED formal notification that I'd been accepted for aviation cadet training. More than five months had elapsed since I'd filed the application. I knew the slots were much sought after, and, I guessed, fairly competitive.

Everything I saw or read confirmed our country's need for airmen. They were glorified in movies, magazines, and posters. Why so long a wait?, I'd fumed. Maybe the funnels were clogged? More trainee applicants than the positions available? Not enough planes or qualified trainers?

Never mind, now. I was in! There was still an extensive set of physical exams designed especially for cadet applicants, and what I recall as another battery of written aptitude exams. But these were a breeze. The nearest thing to a problem arose when I took the tests designed to screen for color blindness.

I was handed a multipage folder of pictures and designs, one to a page, and each comprised of many medium-sized, small, and tiny dots of varied colors, shades, and hues. The dots were so arranged that, woven into the color design of each page, there emerged the shape of an identifiable two-digit number. Its form stood out from the remainder of the pattern solely because of the color of the dots comprising the numbers' shapes.

It was my job to flip through the book, page by page, and call out the number as quickly as I discerned it. Things were going swimmingly. I began taking pride in the rapidity with which I was making the identifications. Suddenly, the examiner said, "Stop."

Then he instructed, "Look at that last one again."

Focusing on the design a second time, I said, "Yes, Sir, it's clear. It's twenty-si—wait a minute! There's *another* number. It's fifty-four!"

He smiled, nodded. "That's right."

He explained that there were *two* numbers blended into the arrangement of each page. One of the numbers was apparent to people with perfect color perception. Someone who is color-blind will see the *other* number, which is composed not by shades of color but by shades of light and darkness.

I went through the rest of the designs, careful now to look more closely, and missed no others. I'd passed. But I marveled at the skill and ingenuity of whoever had devised such an immaculate testing device.

"How on earth did you come up with that imaginative test?" I asked.

"We can't get any more of them," the supervisor replied. "They were created and produced by the Japanese."

SANTA ANA ARMY AIR BASE, located south of Los Angeles, became for most cadets a place of dread. "Hellhole of the Earth," a few luxuriantly, but not so originally, described it. A more imaginative cohort told me it was a "1,300-acre torture chamber."

The aviation cadets' primary western indoctrination center and ground training school thrived on a demanding schedule. The place was strictly all-business. From reveille at 0600 hours (6 A.M.) to lights out at 2200 hours (ten o'clock at night), the cadet population was kept busy and in a hurry.

We double-timed to, from, and between breakfast, classes, lunch, more classes, dinner, then barracks study until lights out. Wedged into the tight schedule of classes was a hurried daily run and work-out followed by a quick shower and return to uniform.

About every ten days our platoon (or "flight," as they called it here) would draw kitchen police (KP) duty, reporting thirty minutes after reveille, clad in greenish fatigues, to one of the mess halls. All day we'd work fast and furiously to feed and clean up after other cadet flights carrying out their own hurried daily routines. We'd finish about six-thirty or seven in the evening.

Here, however, they didn't call it KP. The brazen euphemism was "Mess Management." On each occasion, a commissioned officer would make us a little speech insisting, solemn as a mule, that this experience was academically beneficial to our career training. "You never know when any given military officer may be called upon to manage a mess," he would say. Our skepticism, though universal, was invariably silent. We just wanted the officer to finish his pep talk so we could get on with it.

Someone had even invented high-sounding names for the specific tasks to which we were severally assigned for the day. The "Sanitation Engineers," for example, were those of us who carried out the garbage cans; lifted and emptied them into large wagon beds of trucks headed, we were told, to hog farms; then we scrubbed the big cans glistening clean, and carried them in to exchange for others which, by now, were full and needing to be emptied. The guys who carried big serving platters of food and beverages to the tables were not "waiters" but "Service Maintenance Supervisors." Those given the responsibility of keeping clean the porches, steps, and outer grounds of the mess halls were "Landscape Architects." Mess management, indeed.

Despite a very few such stretches of credulity, the massive cram-speed ground school education drilled into us at Santa Ana was a marvel. From March of 1942 when the facility was dedicated until the end of that year, Santa Ana graduated 23,470 cadets into advanced pilot, bombardier, and navigator air training.

ALL THOSE ADMITTED to Santa Ana at that stage had to have completed at least two years of college in order to handle its curriculum. We had all volunteered for the training and were eager to absorb it. Most of us, I'm convinced, were sensible enough to understand at some level, that our lives, very literally, could depend on how well we learned it.

We mastered the Morse code, something most of us had few occasions to use. But it could be, in exigencies, a lifesaver. We learned map reading, vectoring, and the elements of navigation. Meteorology was, we discovered, of indispensable importance to aircrews. We learned about temperature inversions, updrafts, downdrafts, and wind shear.

We absorbed knowledge of the basic vagaries of nature, and learned how to identify cumulus, stratus, and cumulonimbus clouds. Of the latter, those anvil-shaped nemeses of manned aircraft, we took to heart that sensible summation: *If you can't get over it, or around it, or under it, then get away from it. Go home.* We learned, rehearsed, and practiced identifying at night the positions and juxtapositions of the stars and groupings most essential to nocturnal direction guidance.

We studied and practiced drills on aircraft identification, so that we could quickly recognize the silhouettes of enemy warplanes. We learned of their relative speeds, their maneuverability, their armor, and what firepower they carried.

In one course, we practiced reading aerial photographs, trying to learn how to identify the presence of camouflaged objects. British Intelligence had perfected a physical technique, more art than science but nonetheless highly functional, that allows a skilled practitioner to see the three-dimensional aspect in a flat photo.

Roughly put, you take two identical photographic copies, holding one in each hand, careful only that they coordinate in the same upright position. Then you stare off, both eyes open, not at any object but at some amorphous point in space. So staring, you begin to maneuver the two upright photographs slowly in and out near the lower periphery of your line of sight until you have the two so aligned that they blend and become one photograph instead of two. One picture. At this point, you can see it three-dimensionally, detecting height and depth.

It works, but one learns to do it only through practice. Though all of us had tested at better than 20/20 vision, a lot of the fellows never perfected this particular technique.

On graduating from Santa Ana after three intensive months, the best students among us felt that we'd assimilated a greater load of immediately usable skills and knowledge than in our best full year of college. We'd gained something else, too. Confidence! There was the feeling that, having survived Santa Ana, we could handle anything.

Our flight was on its way to Williams Field, Arizona—a base devoted expressly to the advanced aerial training of pilots and bombardiers.

ON OUR FIRST MORNING at Williams Field, we awakened to the insistent humming, droning, and screaming of aircraft engines revving up and alternately idling on the runway. Engineering crews were warming up the engines and adjusting the fuel mix. The AT-6s would be ready for takeoff first thing after breakfast.

Advanced ground school was every bit as demanding, and as efficacious, as the big doses we'd swallowed at Santa Ana. Only now it was *applied* theory, with daily opportunities to use it and test it in the air.

In alternating morning and afternoon sessions, each of us would spend two hours aloft, working the flight problems assigned. Bombardiers memorized the intricacies of the Norden bombsight, learned the ambidextrous feel of its sensitive rotor knobs, and practiced dropping bombs aimed at the centers of whitewashed sets of circles painted on the desert floor.

The Arizona weather was ideal for our purposes. Every day offered great visibility and fine flying weather. It usually was CAVU (the Air Corps acronym for Ceiling and Visibility Unlimited). There was a certain amount of cross-training in those days, anticipating the need to step in and relieve an injured crewman.

We bombardiers discovered the various arts of working with—and anticipating the intentions of—the pilot, reading the wind and drift meters, applying mathematical formulae based on altitude, aircraft speed, wind direction, and bomb size. In the epicenter of concentric white circles on the ground was a small shack of flammable wooden or composition material. To hit the target dead center with the projectile, or as near dead center as possible, was the aim of the exercise. Each time a bomb actually struck the target shack, it would erupt in quick flames, easily visible from the AT-6 flying overhead at altitudes ranging at first from 2,000 to 8,000 feet.

Our progress was measured by "circular error," the average distance from the target circle's center that the bombs actually landed. Whenever one collided dead-on, igniting the flimsy target, everyone aboard would yell, "Shack!" followed by applause and cheers.

It was an emphatic, indescribable thrill, I quickly discovered, to put one smack on target, eliciting the shouts of delight and back-pounding expressions of approbation from the instructor and other student bombardier trainees aboard.

In my first week I was scoring one shack out of eight tries. After six weeks of daily practice, I'd improved to three shacks in each set of nine efforts, and we were dropping from higher altitudes. Consistency was improving, as well, and substantially shrinking the size of the average circular error.

The desire to satisfy one's self-expectations, and the yen to be respected by one's peers, are both powerful motivators. I suppose the more mature and emotionally secure we become, the more the former suffices and the less necessary the latter is to our happiness. I only know that, at this stage in my own development, I craved both.

◉　◉　◉

ONE OF THE LESS remarked-upon effects of World War II was its kind of homogenizing influence on our American culture. This mixing and mingling of so many young folks from every part of America—kids of such varied geographic, educational, occupational, and religious backgrounds—did much to shatter many of the old intellectually confining walls of parochialism and prejudice.

There were five of us in our dormitory bay at Williams Field. We hailed, respectively, from Philadelphia, Northern California, Florida, North Carolina, and Texas. Two of the fellows were married, three of us single. One was Catholic, one Jewish, two of us Protestant, and one never said. We didn't ask. Friends, we accepted one another unconditionally. Turns out his affiliation was Eastern Orthodox.

One day that fall my mother, knowing my penchant for spicy foods, sent me a big jar of freshly home-prepared "kosher" dill pickles. The cucumbers, peppers, and some of the spices had come from her Victory garden. I asked "Red" Weinstein if he'd like to help me sample these delicacies. They smelled like herbs in a strong breeze. Their piquant fragrance teased our salivary glands inviting satisfaction. We sat there on the barracks floor that afternoon and, between us, ate every last pickle.

Another time, a cadet of Greek ancestry named Gus Pappas proudly unveiled a big roll of baklava. I'd never eaten any or even heard of it, but it looked good. Gus offered me what I thought seemed a mighty stingy little bite. Chomping into it, I realized a bigger mouthful would've been too rich to handle. I'd never savored so tasty and succulent a morsel of sweet, sticky, gooey substance. I became an instant fan.

A couple of mischievous Jewish guys from Brooklyn, observing my interest in languages and cultures, undertook to teach me a few phrases in Yiddish. "Just so you can get along if you find yourself sometime in a big Jewish crowd." Eagerly, I committed the phrases to memory and practiced pronunciation until I was satisfied I had it down pat.

Very soon I discovered the trick they'd played on me. I tried one of the salutations on our roommate, "Red" Weinstein, expecting to surprise him. He was surprised, all right. "Good God, Jim, where'd you learn that?" I told him. Red grinned, then told me what I'd said. I don't remember any of the other friendly greetings I'd been taught. I quickly, and purposely, forgot them. What I'd said to Red was, more or less phonetically spelled out, *Zost echen borquist en pisens borscht.* According to his English translation, I'd told him, candidly put, to eat beets and pee beet soup. Glad I hadn't said it to a stranger.

We all were learning, in wondrous ways, the delightful diversity of our country.

# 4

## CHOICES, ASSIGNMENTS, AND ORDERS

JOHN MOISAN OF CALIFORNIA occupied the bunk next to mine. We found several interests in common. John had played halfback in high school and junior college and had once considered coaching as a likely career. He was interested in the same sporting events as I, read a lot (when time allowed), stayed up with current events, and had a lively attachment to what was going on in the world. John was a couple of years my senior and married. Phyllis, his wife, wrote to him almost daily. I thought I detected a rise or fall in John's disposition depending on whether or not there was a letter from Phyllis at Mail Call.

Most of us, I guess, were similarly affected. Mail Call was the high point in our day. It was our individual hold on reality, our consoling reminder that this time, too, would pass, and we'd be reunited with all the familiar and beloved sights and sounds and smells and feelings that memory associated so tenderly with the places and people we loved the most.

Letters from home were the fuel that reinflated sagging spirits. Dad would write a couple of times weekly—one pithy, punchy, humorous, or philosophically inspired page, hammered out on his portable typewriter. He often enclosed clippings covering events or people I knew or subjects he thought would interest me. Mother wrote weekly, longer epistles inscribed by hand, more folksy and gossipy and feelings-oriented.

Both my parents loved poetry. My fourteen-year-old sister, Mary Nelle, was composing verse now and sent me several of her original compositions—some funny, some sad, some a blend of both. Betty Lee, at twelve, vacillated between tomboy and debutante. She was still trying to find herself. She wrote a lot about summer camp and band practice.

Mary Ethelyn Lemons (everyone called her "Mab") and I corresponded regularly. During the past two years in college we'd gone mostly steady, and for this near-year of absence considered ourselves alternately engaged, or engaged-to-be-engaged. During my two semesters at University of Texas, she'd attended Texas Wesleyan where she was the acknowledged standout in drama, just as she had been during our two years at Weatherford College. Her most distinguishing features were her large, very expressive and very blue eyes.

Popular with both sexes, she could be a bit forbidding to some of the guys. Mab didn't tease. She didn't taunt. She was what we fellows called "a *nice* girl." That, among other attributes, appealed to me. She wasn't someone to play around with. There were plenty of those. She was someone to settle down with.

We had talked of marriage—*eventually*. Trouble was, our individual concepts of "eventually" conjured up mental images of two separate time frames. I meant eventually, like after the war, when I was back home and professionally established. I think her notion of eventually was not next week or maybe even next month, but "before next year, for goodness' sake! Before you go off to war, and maybe get shot up or even worse—and then we'd *never* be together."

The war was, in some ways, a potent aphrodisiac. Wartime marriages blossomed everywhere. There was the feeling that if we cared for one another—really, truly cared—then we deserved the right to share that love, if for but a fleeting moment in time, lest all eternity lament the golden prize unclaimed.

It was not really a very logical argument. But war is not a logical undertaking. Neither, for that matter, is love.

These thoughts were churning in my mind when an orderly charged up the stairs to our second-story barracks bay, calling out, "Cadet Wright! Cadet James Wright!"

"Here I am," I responded.

"You're supposed to report, right now, to Captain Hill!"

"Who," I stammered, "is Captain Hill?"

"One of the senior flight instructors. He wants you there on the double!"

It was almost time for evening chow. This was not only puzzling, but slightly irritating as well.

"Where do I find Captain Hill?" I asked. The orderly gave me an office number in Base Operations, on the flight line. Mystified, I hustled over there, wondering, *What have I done?*

When I entered the office, the captain was sitting at a desk looking down at some papers.

"Cadet Wright reporting, Sir!" I said. I was standing at attention, saluting.

"Why in hell didn't you tell me you were here at Williams?" demanded the captain, suddenly looking up.

I was stunned. Unbelieving.

"Beany?" I blurted. "What the hell? You're a *captain*?"

"What's so strange about that?" grinned Marcus Lee (Beany) Hill.

Beany Hill, who played left guard on the Weatherford College football team. Beany Hill of Cisco, Texas. The Cisco Kid, some of us called him. Beany Hill, who was inseparable on campus from pretty little Joanne Parks.

We were pounding each other on the back before I realized this was not really very military.

"We're having dinner tonight," Beany—I mean, Captain Hill—announced. "It's all arranged!"

"Well, sure! Count me in," I agreed. "But, where—"

"At my house!" he proclaimed with pride. "Joanne was as surprised as I was to read in the *Weatherford Herald* that you were out here."

"Joanne—?"

"Well, hell yes, Joanne. Who'd ya think? We're married! Been married for eight months. This is the life, man! She can't wait to see ya!"

Captain Hill drove a five-year-old coupe that he said he'd bought for four hundred dollars, taking us out through the main gate, saluting the sentries, and the very few miles into nearby Chandler, where he pulled up in the driveway beside a nice little white frame house.

Joanne came running to the door. She looked radiant. Actually, homespun radiant. She unselfconsciously wore an apron. Just enough tiny freckles to be the girl next door, or your sister, but enough good looks and curves to make you glad that she wasn't. "What's a nice girl like you doin' way out here," I asked, "shacking up with this guy who's impersonating an officer? Don't you know that's a federal offense?"

"If he's impersonating a captain, then I'm impersonating a major," she shot back in perky repartee. "Didn't you know a wife always ranks one grade above her husband?"

I did know that, of course. That's a relic of military gallantry that must trace back to the days of knighthood.

But a captain! Already. Beany had entered the Air Corps only about eight or nine months before I did. In those days, with the credentials we both had, you could go straight into aviation cadets. No waiting around.

Beany told me he'd heard that one of our three friends who'd gone into the Canadian Air Force the previous year was already a lieutenant colonel. Right place at the right time. Supply and demand.

But none of us was obsessed with rank that evening. It was so indescribably great to see someone from home!

As we ate and talked—she'd cooked pork chops—I couldn't help noticing how visibly, naturally, giddily happy they both were. Right here in the middle of this godawful huge war and him sure to be on his way overseas soon. These two whom I'd known pretty well on our small-town college campus—whatever lay ahead—were just deliriously, unfeignedly happy! And in love. Just like everybody ought to be, I thought.

It was there, in the reflected glow of their so obvious joy, that I began to be haunted by thoughts of how nice it would be.

*Why not?* I thought. Mother and Dad were married during wartime. She'd been escorted personally by Reverend Dr. John Reeves, Weatherford's Presbyterian minister who would perform the ceremony, all the way to Valentine, in the Davis Mountains where Dad commanded the Weatherford National Guard Company. That unit, along with others, had been federalized by order of President Woodrow Wilson. Their job was to guard the international border during the Mexican Revolution and to keep Pancho Villa's only minimally disciplined revolutionary troops on their side of the Rio Grande.

Almost immediately had come World War I. Mother had followed Dad to Camp Bowie, and to his next assignment in Spartanburg, South Carolina. During his time commanding an infantry company in France, she had lived for a while, at their invitation, with Colonel MacAdams's wife and family on Far Rockaway, Long Island. MacAdams had been Dad's battalion commander. I'd grown up hearing those romantic tales of that romantic time.

Mother had played the piano often in the evenings while the rest of us stood around and sang. From my earliest days I had been familiar with the words and music of World War I–era songs. "Over There," "There's a Long, Long Trail A-Winding," "It's a Long Way to Tipperary," "Give My Regards to Broadway," and a lot of lesser-known ones like "Jeannine, I Dream of Lilac Time" and "The Rose of No Man's Land."

My mother and father had found such nostalgic delight in the playing and singing of these old tunes that I must have imagined war and romance—for all war's hideous hates and atrocities—to be inextricably, and intoxicatingly, interwoven.

There was, of course, one salient difference. Dad was, when they married, twenty-five years old. In a few days, I'd be twenty. But, then, I reminded myself I had always been ahead of my age group. When I was ten, I had tried to join the Boy Scouts. In those days, the minimum age was twelve. At thirteen, I'd wanted to box in the district AAU tournament. The rule was that contestants under sixteen could participate only with written parental consent. It would have been too embarrassing to walk up in front of the other guys with a consent form in my hand. I told the officials I was sixteen. I won the first two bouts and lost the third on a close decision. Having skipped two grades in school, I was always chronologically younger than my classmates—and always secretly apprehensive that someone might find out.

From all of this, I had developed my own private philosophy about age. It was less a matter of chronology than of maturity, I rationalized. Age was relative. Therefore, I concluded that I was the best—and the only competent—authority on how old I actually was. Nearing my twentieth birthday, I was aware that most of the guys in the cadet flight thought I was already twenty-one or more. That suited me just fine.

These negative considerations resolved, it was only a question of whether I was ready to take a wife, to have that responsibility right now. What if I didn't come back? But that really wasn't a major factor in my calculations—unless we were foolish enough, or careless enough, to have a baby. I wouldn't want to leave Mab with a fatherless child. But we knew the rules of the game and I had an overpowering faith that I would return.

Could I support a wife? I entertained no doubt of that. We both were children of the Depression. We'd watched our parents make ends meet. In a time of economic adversity, my father had abolished the word "can't" from the family vocabulary. His spoken creed: "Jim, you can do anything in the world you want to do, if you want it strongly enough, and if you're willing to pay the price."

We graduated on December 12. I had my wings, my gold bars as a second lieutenant, had bought myself a uniform, and soon would have my orders. There was a new heavy bomb group forming up at Davis-Monthan Air Base near Tucson. It was a B-24 outfit, the 380th. Along with most of the men in our flight—in fact, most of the entire cadre that had come to Williams from Santa Ana—I was assigned to report there. They needed bombardiers.

Before our troop train even arrived at Tucson—while it stopped for water at some way station in Arizona—I hopped off long enough to send a telegram.

It told Mab I had bars on my shoulders, wings on my chest, and a ring in my pocket, and invited her to meet me in Tucson.

# 5

## FUN, FATE, AND FAITH

MAB'S TRAIN ARRIVED at the Tucson station on Christmas Eve. We found a Methodist preacher named Folsom who married us. I had rented a small apartment, consisting of a room and a half plus bath. It was in a tourist court named Sage and Sand, on the far side of Tucson from the air base. As in every military town, rooms were scarce. And, by my reckoning, expensive. John and Phyllis Moisan found a similar place nearby.

My bride had brought a small alarm clock, a toaster, and a coffeepot. For the moment those constituted our total family dowry. But, operated in tandem, they sufficed. Since I needed to report in for an early formation every morning at 8:00, we'd set the alarm for 6:15. While I showered, shaved, and dressed, Mab would make toast in the toaster, soft-boil three eggs (one for her and two for me) by bringing water to boil in the coffeepot, then arrange the eggs with the toast while the double-service coffeepot perked us up some coffee.

I'd leave at 7:20, hurry down on foot to the nearest bus stop, transfer once in midtown to a bus serving Davis-Monthan, and arrive in time for formation. Sometimes even six or seven minutes early.

I'd usually phone Mab before leaving the base in those early days at about five in the afternoon. She'd hop a bus and meet me

downtown for a movie or a window-shopping tour, and, occasionally, dinner at a great French restaurant near the big, old western-
style hotel on the downtown corner.

On Friday or Saturday evenings we'd often join some of the
other couples at the officers' club on base. Sunday evenings we'd go
to Reverend Folsom's church. It all was, for the two of us, a grand
adventure.

Soon Mab was acquainted with a dozen or so of the other officers'
wives. These young women, for the wide geographic diversity of their
upbringings, wasted no time at all in discovering the encompassing
unity of the life they now had in common. We had made them, like
"the colonel's lady and Mrs. O'Grady," sisters under the skin.

While the girls got acquainted with one another on their own
time, each of us as a member of an aircrew was getting acquainted
with the other men assigned to our soon-to-be tightly knit unit.
And all of us were getting as intimately acquainted as possible with
the big flying boxcar of an airplane that was to be our wings of
flight, our defense and our refuge from hostile fire, our arsenal of
strength, and our home sweet home in times of adversity.

The B-24 Liberator had the longest range of any bomber at the
time. With four fourteen-cylinder engines, each capable of 1,200
horsepower, the plane could hit 290 miles per hour, or cruise at
about 180 and, fully fueled, fly 2,100 miles before landing.

It carried ten 50-caliber machine guns, could handle 8,000
pounds of bombs, had a top turret and a tail turret, as well as gunnery installed in the nose compartment from which the bombardier
aimed and released the bombs. Fully loaded, the B-24 could weigh
up to 70,000 pounds.

The Liberator's silhouette would not look like a particularly large
airplane today, but to us in 1943 it seemed big, with its 110-foot
wingspan, its 67-foot fuselage, and its distinctive twin tail assembly.

We prowled it, studied it, flew and tested it, and feeling more
and more familiar with it, finally came to love it.

◉ ◉ ◉

WITHIN A SHORT WHILE after the assignment of crews, we began flying night formations and practicing joint bombing runs. It was cold above the desert at night in January, and we were flying at higher and higher altitudes that required wearing our oxygen masks. We'd be bundled up in those big, bulky sheepskin-lined leather suits, communicating by radio between crews as we practiced close and loose formations and coordinated bomb runs on simulated targets underneath.

It was good that the wives were getting to know one another. It saved them lots of lonely days and nights. Sometimes a group of them would arrange joint waiting parties when we first began the night-training exercises. Then, those missions grew longer with cross-country flying assignments, and married crewmen were on their own to find transportation to their off-base quarters after midnight. Luckily for me and most of the married officers, the city buses still ran.

Crews were developing their own camaraderie and team spirit. I liked most of the fellows with whom I flew. A sense of interdependence was sprouting among us. Lieutenant Colonel William A. Miller, in his midthirties and a veteran American Airlines command pilot with more than 7,000 hours of flight time under his belt, inspired a general sense of confidence as our newly designated group commander.

Nightly for several consecutive evenings, we'd fly bombing runs at the bomb range near Alamogordo, New Mexico. The crewmen all, from pilot Gus Connery of Rhode Island to tailgunner Don Greenwood of Massachusetts, shared my pride and cheered me lustily each time we scored a "shack."

Gus was a pleasant, likeable, even-tempered, competent, and personally modest aircraft commander whom everybody instinctively liked and intuitively respected. It became clear to all of us that Pat Mullins, our Boston navigator, and aircraft engineer Tally Koumarelos, whom Gus personally chose after a predecessor candidate had failed to measure up, knew what they were doing.

This mutual confidence grew as Colonel Miller subjected us to increasingly difficult assignments, some in downright bitchy weather. The ubiquitous rumor mill was rollicking with predictions that we were being trained for high-altitude flights over Germany, or possibly the CBI (China-Burma-India) Theater, where we'd be "flying the Hump." Consensus was that we were headed for somewhere with long nights and lousy weather. One wiseacre even surmised that we were being prepared to fly out of Alaska to attack Japan across the Aleutians chain. Idle chatter, but better than none at all.

IN ARMY AIR CORPS JARGON, what we were going through was "phase training." There were three distinct phases to our regimen. Phase two began when the group moved to Biggs Field at El Paso, where we spent some of January and most of February practicing and perfecting the arts we'd rehearsed. The emphasis now was on coordinating our individual efforts into functional teamwork, like the fingers of a hand becoming a fist.

Our growing confidence in a common invincibility was rudely shaken by two separate calamities that occurred on the very same night in February. Two of our 530th squadron teammates, pilot Oscar Cantrell and navigator John Gessenger, both second lieutenants, died while trying to ride a burning B-24 to a safe landing. The fire had started in the cockpit. When efforts to extinguish it failed, Cantrell told the rest of the crew to bail out, and they did, parachuting to the ground about twenty miles north of El Paso.

Eight other colleagues also went to their deaths that night when a 528th plane carrying out a high-altitude flight suffered carburetor icing at 20,000 feet above Roswell, New Mexico. Controls locked, and the B-24 went into a vertical spin. Pilot Charles Wylie was unable to pull it out, and it crashed, nose-down, into the desert. Only one man—Staff Sergeant Ralph King—managed to bail out.

On that morning of February 20, for our gaggle of guys, war lost a little bit of its luster. We'd each had other reminders of this war's harsh reality, and would have more. With each, its shining glory dimmed just a shade. Our cause was just—no one doubted that. But it was ceasing to be glamorous. On that day, for our friends, and friends of friends, war was grim.

The group's chaplain, Reverend Harry Roark of Duncan, Oklahoma, worked overtime that week. He sensed the need to visit quietly with all those closest to our dead colleagues. To contact and console their families, to let other members of their squadrons vent their sorrow, or anger, or whatever emotions were building up inside them, became his work. In the course of my watching him do this, I developed an admiration for Roark that grew into a friendship. Although I hadn't known him then, as a youth of eleven, I had lived in his hometown, and he, a Baptist, had attended seminary in Fort Worth at Southwestern Baptist, perhaps at that time America's largest theological seminary.

Fresh on the minds of us all was the heroic nationally publicized episode, only eighteen days earlier, of the four chaplains—a Catholic priest, a Jewish rabbi, a Methodist minister, and a Dutch Reformed clergyman—who'd worked hand in hand and ultimately, voluntarily given their own lives to save others. When the USA transport *Dorchester* was sunk by a German U-boat in the icy waters south of Greenland on February 3, the chaplains had made a pact to save as many personnel as possible. They'd done this, helping young fellows into lifeboats and even giving away their own seats and life jackets, at one point their gloves. They willingly forfeited their own chances of survival to save young American servicemen.

This was, for me and millions of others, an inspiring example of the unifying spirit that was joining America together in those days of 1942 and early '43. There'd been few military victories to cheer. But each triumph of the spirit emboldened and strengthened us.

IN THIS ENVIRONMENT, fed by a torrent of rising public indignation over the inhumane atrocities committed by the Nazis against Central Europe's Jewish minority, there grew across America a revival of simple and unashamed religious faith, tempered by a growing spirit of ecumenism. I'm not aware that anyone gave a name to this phenomenon, but it was palpable.

As one wag put it, Americans would fight to the death to protect everybody's right to worship at a church they stayed away from, or to stay away from the church they worshipped at. But, actually, I believe it was both deeper and broader than this. Two years earlier, in January of 1941, President Roosevelt and Prime Minister Churchill met "somewhere in the Atlantic," worshipped together aboardship on a Sunday morning, and proclaimed a future world devoted to universalizing the Four Freedoms: freedom of speech; freedom of worship; freedom from want; freedom from fear.

It was an almost evangelical call to which American public opinion rallied—a sort of divine commission to see that nobody on earth anymore would wear a shackle or drag a chain, live in fear or starve; and that all God's human creatures would have a chance at not only the legal freedoms but also the basic physical necessities that we, ourselves, enjoyed. One cynic derisively labeled it "Milk for the Hottentots," but most Americans bought into it. Norman Rockwell, who was to painting what Bing Crosby was to popular music, produced four covers for the *Saturday Evening Post*, each extolling one of the Four Freedoms in ordinary life.

Our growing national zeal had a vaguely, if not distinctly, spiritual flavor. This was 1943, remember, in the steaming cauldron of war. Our generally Jeffersonian concept of religious freedom, unlike the court-sanctioned version that would develop forty and fifty years later, was still more concerned with the freedom *to* worship than with the freedom *from* worship.

World heavyweight boxing champion Joe Louis had taken a wartime absence from the ring so that he could enlist in the military service and give his full-time energies to the war effort. It was his religious, as well as patriotic, duty, the champion opined. A radio interviewer asked if Louis thought God was on our side. The Brown Bomber said he thought it more important to be sure we stayed on God's side.

"Praise the Lord and Pass the Ammunition" was the title of what became a popular song on the radio charts. It sprang from a real-life event, in which a naval chaplain took over the machine-gun position from a wounded sailor and continued firing effectively at oncoming enemy aircraft. Another sentimental ballad popular that year was "Coming In on a Wing and a Prayer," inspired by an Air Corps fighter pilot who'd lost an engine to enemy bombardment. A popular best-selling book was written by longtime Air Corpsman, Colonel Robert L. Scott, who had flown with General Claire Chennault in China. It was titled *God Is My Co-Pilot*.

All this was part of the fermenting culture of the '40s. It served American unity in its encompassing character. Old religious rivalries between Catholics, Protestants, and Jews—which at moments in our history had threatened to spill over into the American political arena—were for the duration shelved, trumped by the all-embracing principles we Americans were now openly celebrating.

Unity. That was the watchword. General Eisenhower was struggling to promote it with our allies in Europe. In our case, here at Biggs Field, it extended down to the crew level. Or, I guess, that's where it had to start—and percolate up from there.


A CREW WAS NOT JUST ten separate individuals. We were a unit. A team. Our ten began to realize we had to depend on each other, little by little discovering that we could—on the ground as well as in the air. While there in El Paso, everyone wanted to go, at least once, across the international border into Juarez, Mexico. On one February morning, two of our crewmen failed to show up for the early flight-line formation. I was summoned to the operations room where an unexpected telephone call awaited me. It was one of our missing crewmen.

"Hey, Tex, we're in the hoosegow! I mean, Lieutenant! They say our commanding officer has to come over here before they'll let us out."

"That's not me," I reminded him. "That'd be Connery, or maybe they mean Miller." (A rawboned captain named Fred Miller—not to be confused with Colonel William Miller—at that time was our squadron commander. He was sometimes irreverently referred to, outside his hearing, as "Fearless Fred.")

"Jeez, not Miller! For God's sake, Lieutenant, don't tell Captain Miller! I thought you'd know what to do, bein' from Texas here, and talkin' Spanish and all."

"Where are you?" I asked.

"Hell, I don't know, Sir," said Sergeant Farley. "We're in Juarez somewhere. We're in the stinkin' jail."

"I'll get Connery," I promised. So Gus and I drove over in a jeep, discussing the predicament. "No point trying to throw our weight around," Connery was saying. We agreed we could all be in trouble if we got into a fracas.

We found the jail easily enough and tried to talk with the Mexican police officer in charge. His English was almost nonexistent, worse than my poor Spanish, and we weren't making much progress. Our two crewmen had been picked up in a street altercation about midnight. They were *muy borracho*, the police officer said. "Very drunk," I translated for Gus, who looked at me and shook his head.

"*Lo sientamos mucho*," I stammered, trying to express our regret. The Mexican officer began saying something about charges and a trial. "*Podemos pagar?*" I asked nervously, offering to pay their fine and reaching in my pocket for emphasis. "*Quanto tarifa?*" I probably had about twenty dollars in cash, at most. I had no idea what Gus was carrying.

At this point, another man walked up, in civilian dress—apparently a commissioner of some kind. The police officer deferred to him. Looking sternly at us, he explained in very good English that one of our men had been whistling at Mexican girls on the street, and had gotten into a shoving match with three young Mexican men who objected. "Your men are lucky that the officers came, because a crowd was gathering and they could have been badly hurt."

Gus explained our situation—that we were almost ready to ship out for combat—and promised to see that there'd be no further trouble if our men were released to our care. The commissioner released them, dismissed the charges without a fine, after making certain we understood that we were guests in their country and their young women were as precious to them as our sisters were to us, and entitled to the same respect.

That was a good lesson, indeed, and we all nodded soberly in assent. On the way back, all four of us in the same jeep, Gus said, "No need to spread this around too much."

"Good Lord, no," I agreed. "Captain Miller and Colonel Miller have too much serious stuff on their minds to be bothered with something like this."

In the backseat, both crewmen grinned big, enthusiastically waving V-for-victory signs. The story would spread, all right—among the enlisted ranks—but it would not be reported to the brass.

After that, I think maybe all of us on the crew realized the degree to which we depended on one another, had to stick up for one another, and owed an intense loyalty, each to the rest. That was the nature of an aircrew.

# 6

## SAINTS, SINNERS, AND CIVILIAN SOLDIERS

NO, WE WEREN'T SAINTS. Far from it. Most of us wouldn't even qualify as "eager beavers," the popular semiderisive term invented for those who polished brass and kissed ass, and tried to outshine their contemporaries to curry favorable notice from those who sat in judgment on promotions in rank and other favors. An "eager beaver" would ostentatiously perform work that didn't need performing to impress people who, if he did his job, shouldn't need impressing.

A bunch of civilians in uniform. That phrase might have described most of us best. Most had little interest in pursuing a military career. We were working for, and looking forward to, two things only: V-Day and an honorable discharge.

One thing that made life more endurable for all the G.I. Joes, citizen soldiers called up (or voluntarily signed up for the "duration and six months") was the near universality of the wartime experience. Neither wealth nor celebrity excused a physically fit young American male from uniformed service.

At Williams Field, I had met All-American footballer Tommy Harmon, an aviation cadet just like me. One day at the Base Exchange at Biggs Field, two of us ran into movie idol Clark Gable.

He wore, in addition to his trademark mustache, an Air Corps captain's uniform and the wings of a trained aerial photographer. He was on his way to combat missions in Europe.

Hollywood star James Stewart had been among the early round of draftees in 1940. He'd uncomplainingly accepted his lot as a $21-a-month army private, but had volunteered, just as our guys had, for flight training. He participated in hazardous combat, ultimately becoming a flight commander and a colonel.

Senator Henry Cabot Lodge Jr. became a tank commander in Africa; Franklin D. Roosevelt Jr. was a gunnery officer on a naval destroyer, and at one point led a commando raid on Makin Island. I got acquainted with a nephew of Senator Leverett Saltonstall, serving in uniform just like the rest of us. As things would develop, all eight American presidents from Dwight D. Eisenhower through George H. W. Bush wore the uniform during World War II, and six of them saw active combat.

The very all-inclusiveness of our wartime effort infused—for the time, at least—a spirit of egalitarianism into the military's essentially caste-ridden culture, supplanting some of the rigidities of rank with a leavening camaraderie of shared experience.

THE 380TH MOVED at the end of February to Lowry Field in Denver for our third and final phase of preparation for overseas assignment. Aircrews flew to Lowry, carrying our personal belongings, carefully tucked into our bulging, hand-carried B-4 bags, aboard our own assigned Liberators, leaving ground personnel to come the next day by troop train from El Paso. Dependents—Mab and the other wives—were on their own to get to Denver. Most of the young wives bought tickets together on the same train, scheduled to arrive on the following afternoon.

That first night in Denver, there were insufficient quarters on base to accommodate our numbers; so most of our air crewmen had been booked in the Brown Palace Hotel, a stately old landmark in the middle of downtown Denver.

It was there (and that very night, I'm tempted to speculate) that the infamously celebrated "Tailhook" parties of a later generation had their inaugural inspiration. A number of the fellows got roaring drunk. Just as our party segued from raucous to riotous, some of our single fellows came in off the streets accompanied by a troupe of Denver's finest "ladies of the night," boldly offering tricks for treats.

At this point, a bombardier (and married) Williams Field classmate of mine named Paul Hebner took umbrage at the flagrant flaunting of their wares by the girls-for-hire. Deciding independently that they were "too hot," Hebner ceremoniously tore a fire extinguisher from an interior wall of the Brown Palace Hotel and began gratuitously "cooling down" the individual ladies with generous sprays of frothy mist from the fire extinguisher canister.

Not surprisingly, some of the unappreciative girls went bananas, and complained to the hotel manager about their ill treatment. The next day, a penitent—and sober—Second Lieutenant Hebner appeared before our group commander, Lt. Col. William Miller. The official dressing-down, according to unofficial group legend, went something like this:

Lt. Col. Miller: "Lieutenant, what in the name of God did you have in your mind when you ripped off the fire extinguisher from the wall and began squirting it on those girls? If you'd gotten that stuff in their eyes, it could've blinded them."

Lt. Hebner: "Sir, I'm sorry, and all I can say, Sir, is that at the time, Sir, it just seemed like a real good idea."

At least, that is the way the colloquy was commonly reported. It had the ring of authenticity.

Thereafter, in Hebner's attributed phraseology, it became—for a while—an acceptable answer to any inquiry as to why someone had done some dumb thing: "At the time, Sir, it seemed like a real good idea."

NO DOUBT WE CIVILIAN SOLDIERS got by with infractions that in the Regular Army would have brought down wrathful retribution on the heads of the offenders. One big reason there weren't more courts-martial in 1942 and '43 was the country's desperate need for the services of us in the training of whom our taxpayers had invested substantial sums and our country's precious time.

The financial investment in one second lieutenant, graduated with his special certified skills from aviation cadet schools, came to a fairly impressive figure at the time. We were often reminded of this in the Army Air Corps's equivalent of locker-room pep talks. Another sum bandied about for our edification was the reputed $366,000 price tag of just one B-24. Maybe these reminders were meant to enhance our self-esteem or our pride of service. If they were meant to discourage us from taking unnecessary risks, we already had a far better reason for that!

One thing most of us liked about the Air Corps was that there was less distracting emphasis on such things as, for example, the dress code. We knew the regulations, and they made no exception for flying personnel. But we indulged certain idiosyncrasies as unwritten prerogatives. One involved the officer's dress hat. We removed the circular grommet which kept it stretched stiff, and let it flop down about our ears. A scarf made of parachute silk was anti-reg and perhaps officially frowned upon, but widely tolerated. Several of us from my part of the country had, on occasion, worn cowboy boots while otherwise faithfully in uniform.

On March 17 of that year, I pushed the envelope almost too far, showing up for duty with a bright green St. Patrick's Day scarf around my neck and stuffed between the lapels of my official short-coat. This drew a gentle reprimand from a captain whom I didn't know. Something like, "You know, Lieutenant, that's really not regulation uniform." I said, "I know, Sir. It's just that it's St. Patrick's Day!" He replied, "So I notice." We were fairly relaxed about that kind of stuff.

SOMETHING ELSE OCCURRED on that particular St. Patrick's Day, of which we were unaware at the time. Back in Washington, a conversation taking place in the White House on that March 17 would profoundly affect the future of the 380th Group.

Major General George C. Kenney, leader of combat flying units in the South Pacific and commander of the newly created 5th Air Force, had arrived in Washington on March 10, summoned there by top Air Corps General Henry H. (Hap) Arnold for a conference on air strategy in the Pacific.

Kenney has written of that particular trip. He specifically recalls an invitation from President Roosevelt on March 17 to come to the White House for a personal talk. There, in response to the president's questioning, Kenney mentioned his pressing need for one full heavy bomb group, preferably with B-24s, to make long-range flights and keep steady pressure on Japanese forces in Java, Sumatra, the Celebes Islands, and Timor. Kenney's goal was to harass and disrupt enemy bases, shipping and supply lines and weaken their resources while we amassed sufficient ground forces for a land assault on enemy positions. Roosevelt promised to "look into the matter," and good-humoredly suggested that "a few airplanes" might be "found somewhere" that could be sent his way.

According to Kenney's memoir, he was called to General Arnold's office on March 22 and told that he was to get one new heavy bombardment group (B-24s), two and a half medium bomb groups (B-25s and B-26s), and three more fighter groups.

At that moment, the 380th's destiny was sealed. Ours was the next B-24 group coming on line of readiness for overseas duty. Kenney returned to Australia on April 6, happy with the results of his trip.

Meanwhile, at the Pentagon, orders had been in the process of being cut that would have sent the 380th to England. Those had to be scrubbed when General Arnold tapped the 380th for Australia. Also, a new set of instructions was filed to make certain that our aircraft were properly configured and equipped with the necessary modifications for the Southwest Pacific theater.

We were at the time oblivious to all of this. Rumors floated around the 380th like tumbleweeds on the western plains. The one that gained the most currency involved assignment to our group of an intelligence officer named Farid Simaika. He spoke fluent Arabic, we were told. On one occasion, he gave a lecture involving the customs, mores, and taboos of Arab culture. Everyone had a clean hand and a dirty hand, we learned. The latter should not be extended in greeting, and a bone-crusher handshake was considered rude. When seated, talking with an Arab, we shouldn't cross our legs in such a way that the soles of our shoes were exposed in the other's direction.

After that day's lecture, most of us were certain our group was headed for North Africa. Who knows? That might have been the Pentagon's original intention—before General Kenney's persuasive conversation with FDR on March 17.

AN OFFICIAL, HIGH-LEVEL inspection party arrived at Lowry on March 30. The announced purpose was to certify the combat readiness of the 380th pilots, navigators, and bombardiers. The inspection methodology was thorough and substantive, not just ceremonial.

General Eugene Eubank, whose current title was AAF Inspector for Bombardment, led the team of professionals. He was already a celebrated veteran of the Pacific War, where he'd been commander of the 19th Bomb Group, based in New Guinea. This might have given us a clue, but nobody cranked that fact into the equation.

A good part of the day was given over to tests and inspections. Discovering only one mathematical error in a groupwide set of navigational exercises, a hard-nosed inspector named Sherer ordered the entire exercise to be repeated. He withheld certification of anyone until every submission and calculation was precisely perfect. It was then we knew these guys were for real.

Col. Miller wanted to impress the inspectors with our professionalism and state of readiness. So we saw them off with an aerial flyover and an honor guard. Our formation flyover went well, I thought, but the close-order drill by the honor guard was a near disaster.

Most of the ones chosen to do the marching had good technical skills and ratings, but didn't know either the marching orders or the manual of arms. Someone said their disparate efforts to carry out the spit-and-polish honors drill looked like a Keystone Kops routine performed by paralytic kangaroos. Like I told you—civilian soldiers.

Then First Lieutenant Howard Merkel, a 528th pilot bringing a B-24 in from the flyover, shot what we commonly called a "hot landing." Just barely clearing the fence at the runway's end, Merkel—as the landing gears took hold of the pavement—thrust this whole weight onto the brakes, like a trick rider rising in his saddle to stand with his body weight thrown onto the balls of his feet in the stirrups, while pulling back on the reins. As the Liberator slowed, nose low, the pilot executed a quick turnoff onto a taxiway.

The general, surprised by the deft, unorthodox maneuver and negatively disposed to "showboating," asked Col. Miller to have the pilot report to him immediately on parking the plane.

Facing Merkel, Eubank demanded to know just what the lieutenant thought he was doing. Merkel's aplomb and quick ingenuity were thereafter widely cited, the pilot's answer quoted within our group by chroniclers of the conversation. "Sir," Lt. Merkel said, "they tell me most airfields in those combat zones are extremely short. I've been trying to practice the kind of landings we'll probably have to be doing out there very soon."

The general, apparently admiring the young lieutenant's initiative and originality, thanked him and dismissed him.

It was then that he turned, shook his head, and exclaimed to his inspection team: "My God, these men are a flying circus."

And that is how we got our name. And our certification.

# 7

## SENTIMENTAL JOURNEY

WITH OUR FINAL CERTIFICATION, thirteen days after General Kenney's visit with President Roosevelt, we were officially "combat ready," and, though most of us didn't know it quite yet, Australia-bound.

Col. Miller declared a three-day pass to let each of us go home for a final visit with our families before leaving for overseas duty. We were all to report back at Lowry on April 3.

It was a fond and warm but too-brief moment of family reunion after more than a year's absence. Mab did not come back to Weatherford with me, electing instead to stay there in Denver, where our rented quarters were paid up. She would see me off from there on our final embarkation. It would be an extravagance, she insisted, to buy an extra ticket for her to Fort Worth and back.

"We can save it up and use it for a bassinet when you come back!" she said with a grin.

I looked at her in shocked surprise.

"Are you telling me you're—" I stammered.

"No, not now, silly! I mean when you come back from overseas!"

◉ ◉ ◉

IN WEATHERFORD, I NOTICED first that Dad and Mother had plowed a portion of the spacious west lawn and planted a neat, well-kept Victory garden. The big old Victorian house sat on a quarter of the city block with a decorative wrought-iron fence around the property, just two blocks from the southwest corner of the Court House Square.

I knew Mother had canned fruits and vegetables the previous summer and fall. She had sent me jars of pickles and watermelon-rind preserves, my favorites. It was estimated somewhere that almost 40 percent of the vegetables consumed domestically that year had been harvested from home Victory gardens.

Mary Nelle shared some of her latest poetry with me, and I listened appreciatively as Betty Lee performed several pieces she'd mastered on the piano.

Whenever I thought of Mother, several images always came to mind: her sewing machine, her piano, her canning apparatus, some of the culinary specialties she knew I liked best, and, of course, her books. In her youth, before her marriage, she had taught poetry and English literature. She still enjoyed doing book reviews for the local Women's Club.

That night, at my urging she sat down at the piano and played some of the old family favorites as the rest of us stood around and sang along. For me, that was a moment of delicious nostalgia. Dad's Irish tenor could have been classic, I thought, if he didn't smoke so many cigarettes. On old standbys like "My Wild Irish Rose" and "Let Me Call You Sweetheart," I'd try the lead and he would fill in with the tenor harmony. No doubt many could have found ample flaws in our lusty efforts, but by Mother's long-standing edict, nobody in this family was allowed to criticize another's singing. Whatever its imperfections, Mother was convinced that the human voice was the world's most versatile musical instrument. The only thing better, she'd say, were two or more voices blended in harmony. Her sentimental favorite duets were those by Jeanette MacDonald and

Nelson Eddy. They were the best of all, she'd insist—always adding, "Except, of course, for family."

Dad and I talked into the night about the war, military service, local politics, and business. I had a chance to tell him (I'd regretted not having done so before) how I treasured all the gifts, tangible and intangible, that he'd given me over the years. I remarked in particular about the message he'd had engraved on the watch he'd presented to me on the day I graduated from high school.

In that year of my graduation, 1939, the Great Depression was still much in evidence. Our family was just beginning to claw a foothold on the road to recovery. If I had dared to think at all of a graduation gift, my expectation would have been modest.

My surprise was complete that day when my father called me in and opened a gift box bearing the name of a jeweler. Sparkling against its velvet setting was this very beautiful watch, thin as a wafer, its second hand as silent as the falling snow. It had cost, I was told, fifty dollars . . . much too much for any watch, except maybe this one.

Then Dad did, for him, an unusual thing. He had never before made me a gift with strings attached. This time there was one qualification. "I want you to promise," he said, "that each time you look at the face of this watch, you'll think of the words inside the back cover."

Carefully, I took the watch in my hands and opened the back. Inscribed there were the words: LEAD US NOT INTO TEMPTATION, BUT DELIVER US FROM EVIL.

What a relentless admonition for a clock! There followed years in college, a newfound freedom from parental restraints. Evenings after books were closed, weekends in the zestful atmosphere of a state university, various diversions suggested by the restless young. Instinctively one looks at his watch to see if there's time. Each time I looked upon it, the words whispered themselves to me in the rhythm of its quiet breath . . . "Lead us not into temptation . . . "

War now had come, and like several million others of my generation, I was soon to be in a distant land. The cities would be strange cities; we'd be lonely and maybe a little scared. Who could blame young men who grasped at the fleeting figures of forgetfulness for a moment? But right there in my pocket would be the watch . . . "Deliver us from evil."

I told Dad I'd be taking the watch overseas with me. I thanked him for that lesson, and a lot of others that I hoped I'd remember.

Dad was all heart, but I knew privately that he was part con man. I really didn't mind, and accepted my role as a straight man in these family dramas. Whenever he conned me into doing something, I knew it was for *my* benefit, not his.

The year I was fourteen, for example, he had asked me if I'd do him a favor. There was a new book he was thinking of buying for each of the salesmen in his company, he explained (with a straight face), and he wondered if I would mind reading it for him and advising him on whether I thought it was worthy of sending to his sales force.

Huh? Me? Me, fourteen. *Me* advise *him*? I knew, of course, what was in Dad's mind. He'd probably already read the book. He wanted *me* to read it, and carefully enough to discuss some of its passages with him. The book was *How to Win Friends and Influence People*, by Dale Carnegie.

I read and enjoyed it, and gave the book a positive review. I learned a lot of things from it. But Dad? He could've written the book. Sometimes, I thought I could read him like a book. More important, I knew, was that he could almost always read me.

This day, as we sat talking in the cool of the evening and listening to a cheerful mockingbird recite his joyous repertoire, Dad said, "Jim, you've got a strong admirer in George Fant, in case you didn't know it."

Dad's friend, Mr. Fant, was president of Weatherford's First National Bank, and arguably the town's most prominent citizen. George's son, Knox, on whom the father doted, had been killed in action a few months earlier, and Dad said George was having a hard time surmounting his grief and reconciling his mind to how such a promising life could have come, in the cosmic fitness of things, to such a premature and violent end.

I knew both Fants, of course, father and son. Knox Fant, about six or seven years my senior, had been exemplary in all things—a scholar, an athlete, a winsome personality, and an all-around decent man. Learning of his death back in the fall while I was at Williams Field, I had written the elder Fant a personal letter of condolence, telling him how much Knox's good example had meant to a lot of us younger fellows.

On the next day, as I knew Dad was trying to suggest, I went by the bank to pay my respects to the elder Fant. In my sophomore college year, Harold Owen and I had borrowed $50 from him to buy a ten-year-old Model A Ford coupe. A year later, my classmate Bob Lott and I borrowed $300 to buy some Karakul lambs, which we'd raised on his parents' ranch, selling the grown sheep for about a $150 profit after returning the loan. My experiences with the largest of our town's three banks had been pleasant.

Well, *almost* uniformly pleasant. When I'd landed my after-school job with the Texas Attorney General, in my junior year, my pay was thirty dollars a month. I considered that amount too much to cash all at once and carry around in my pocket. So I had deposited the monthly checks into my personal checking account at Mr. Fant's bank. Against that princely sum, I'd write small checks—often for only a dollar—enough to take care of daily incidentals.

There was a snag. On the walking route between my rooming house and the campus was an establishment known as Charlie's Liquor Store. A prominent sign in the window one day caught my eye. It proclaimed: WE GLADLY CASH STUDENTS' CHECKS! The spirit of that message appealed to me. Especially did I like Charlie's use of the word "gladly." It bespoke a very welcoming attitude.

Thereafter, I gave Charlie most of my check-cashing business. I bought hardly any of his wares (a pint bottle of Bourbon Deluxe cost, as I recall, $1.10), but I did give Charlie a majority of my check-cashing business, because he seemed so graciously accommodating. Many mornings, on my way to campus, I'd step into Charlie's and cash a check for one dollar. I could get eggs and bacon at the corner drugstore for thirty cents, leaving me seventy cents for other contingencies. Charlie was, for all practical purposes, my Austin banker—at the very least, my check-casher.

I'd made one strategic mistake, I suppose, in patronizing the same bank in which my dad kept his own account. One month, as Murphy's Law decreed, the bank made an error. It included my cancelled checks, together with my monthly statement, in the same big envelope with my father's, and he was not happy to observe the percentage of my daily drafts made out to an establishment that dealt in alcoholic spirits!

The next letter I received from my father should have been encased in an asbestos envelope. He advised me in no uncertain terms that (1) he felt no financial obligation to any establishment known as Charlie's Liquor Store; (2) he could not imagine how any student could even attend class while consuming as much of that establishment's wares as reflected in my cancelled checks; and (3) if I was *not* attending class, just to get my anatomy on home!

I'm not sure I ever truly convinced my father that my relationship with Charlie was—shall we say—strictly fiduciary.

But I'd long since forgiven my banker that serious breach of client confidentiality, and now I felt sorry for the kindly old gentleman over the loss of his son, Knox.

George Fant was overjoyed to see me and we exchanged stories. I let him bring up the subject of Knox's death. He did so early in our conversation by thanking me, almost profusely, for my kindness in writing him. He said he still had my letter. I asked him sympathetically how he was faring personally in the aftermath of his tragic loss.

George Fant looked me straight in the eye. "I've learned one thing, Jimmy. You've just gotta go through what you've gotta go through if you're ever gonna get to where you've gotta get to."

I parsed that sentence in my mind and found little in the philosophy that I could question.

In fact, George Fant's dictum kept running through my mind in the remaining three weeks before that night we'd get in our crew's Liberator, rev up the engines, and take off for the Pacific.

Mab and I talked sometimes at night about the upcoming long absence from one another, about our financial plans, my monthly Air Corps allotment to her, our pledge to build a modest savings by buying a war bond every month, our longer-range plans for the future, the eventual bassinet. And, all the while, knowing in our minds the harsh truth of the present:

*You've gotta go through what you've gotta go through if you're ever gonna get to where you've gotta get to.*

# 8

## LONG NIGHT'S FLIGHT FROM HOME

IN THE LATE EVENING of April 24, 1943, the first of twenty-nine B-24 bombers, manned by skeleton crews, lifted off from the airstrip at Hamilton Field, just north of San Francisco. We were en route to Hickam Field, Hawaii, where we hoped to put down at about 7:30 the next morning. We flew singly, not as a formation. Takeoffs were scheduled five minutes apart.

This was the first of five legs in the overseas movement of the 380th Heavy Bomb Group, known to a small circle within the Army Air Corps as "The Flying Circus." We were four squadrons, each consisting of nine planes and crews.

Seven elite crews, including that of Group Commander Miller, had preceded us by two or three days. Our crew, part of the 530th Squadron, would land eight days later at Amberley Field near Brisbane, Australia, the final destination of our almost 10,000-mile journey.

Eager as we'd been to get into the action, that first night was, for me and for most of us, a tense and anxious one. The long over-water flight in the dark was a new experience, throbbing with adventure and fraught with uncertainties. There I was, at age twenty, a second lieutenant trained as a bombardier with some cross-training in navigation and metrology and maybe forty hours of "stick time," certified as "combat ready," embarking on this first night leg of our journey into the Pacific combat zone.

Like most of the others in our group, I'd never flown anywhere nearly this far over water, nor so far in the dark with no view of earth below. Of the four classic forms of navigation we'd studied, two were completely off the table for this journey.

It was impossible to radio ahead for instructions or to get a directional fix on a radio beam. All of our bases in the mid-Pacific were maintaining absolute radio silence, which forbade any effort to contact Hickam or any point en route. "Pilotage"—the plotting of a course by visual observation and orientation with landmarks— was out of the question, too. It was dark as pitch, and there simply weren't any landmarks. Nothing but shoreless miles of ocean.

Even dead reckoning—our oft-practiced discipline of setting a compass heading and crabbing into the wind just enough (as figured by vectors drawn on a piece of graph paper) to compensate for the wind's force and direction—was compromised. There was no way to know the direction and velocity of winds at our altitude after we'd left the coastal zone for which weather forecasters had briefed us back at Hamilton Field. This was before the day of radar equipment, and even our drift meters were useless, as the very waves below were in constant movement.

The only reliable check upon our compass, or proof of our precise location en route, was in the heavens. Our twenty-four-year-old navigator, Pat Mullins of Boston, kept his handheld sextant busy taking "fixes" on the recognizable stars to reassure us that we weren't being blown off course. Pat was good at what he did. At thirty-minute intervals, he would "triangulate" our precise position on planet Earth by drawing straight lines from each of three heavenly bodies, plotting our own moving location. When the three lines intersected at the same point in our path, we all breathed easier. At least we knew exactly where we were. Gus Connery, our pilot, would make corrections whenever the stars showed us that vagabond winds had blown us four or five degrees off course.

There were six of us in the "skeleton" crew—pilot, copilot, navigator, bombardier, flight engineer, and radio operator. During the long moments between navigational fixes that night, each of us was alone with his private thoughts in those deep mental silences that somehow surmounted the hypnotic drone of four propeller engines.

As the dark night swallowed us and we inched farther and farther west above the broad ocean, our minds drifted back, clutching past images—the last embrace with loved ones, the fond and funny things of home—then lurching into the unknowable future, I trying to embed in my memory the silhouette shapes of all the Japanese military aircraft—the Zekes, the Zeros, the Rufes, the Jakes—then, always springing back to the pregnant present, straining our eyes to perceive the illusory outline of any island chain, anywhere amid the miles of ocean still in front of us.

Maybe what made the night a nervous one for us all was really the subliminal awareness of broader uncertainties ahead. We all covered such doubts as we had with bravado. The tension evaporated as the first fingers of sunrise, tinting the sky faintly behind us, began to light up the path ahead. Suddenly, there on the horizon before us at one o'clock loomed the dim outline of an island. It was the easternmost of the Hawaiian chain. Broad smiles lighted all our faces. Later, each admitted to the others that, for all our feigned confidence, we'd been "just a little uneasy." Scared as hell might have been more like it.

# 9

## SWEET LEILANI

AS SOON AS OUR PLANE was parked off the runway and safely chocked by the Hickam ground contingent, we checked into the barracks reserved for visiting crews and slept for five hours or so. I dreamed of the wedding we'd witnessed the previous evening before leaving Hamilton. A young copilot in our squadron named Richard St. Dennis was married in the base chapel to a beautiful, handsomely dressed blonde girl. There followed a reception at the officers' club attended by the young woman's parents. Affable hosts, they'd appeared deliriously happy with the situation. From their dress and demeanor, I guessed the parents to be people of some prominence. The event seemed a bit bizarre, held just hours before takeoff with no notion as to when—dared I think *whether?*—the groom would return. Bizarre, yes, and arguably impractical, but touchingly beautiful—and so sentimentally in tune with the times. Dream stuff fit for a Hollywood screenplay.

I awakened thinking about my own bride of four months. Mab, my college sweetheart of almost three years, and I had said our vows in Tucson on the previous Christmas Day. She had accompanied me thereafter to each of our destinations of phase training, making a temporary one-room home in a hotel or tourist court as near as possible to the air base. Many other young wives were doing the same.

There was something a little wild and crazy, but terribly romantic, about the rash of weddings that took place in those socially aberrant war years. Young women wanted to be a part of our single-minded national obsession which the war had become. I could not define just what drove our impulse to marry amid such unsettled conditions. But it was all hopelessly romantic and very wonderful.

After awakening and dressing, Gus, Pat, copilot Bob Russell, and I jeeped over to the plane and talked with the ground crew. Sergeant Tally Koumarelos, our aircraft engineer, was already there. He had already gone over the entire plane with almost microscopic precision, and everything seemed to be in good working order, he assured us. "When did you sleep?" Gus asked. The big Greek laughed. "Couple of hours ago," he replied.

As soon as we checked with Major Forrest Brissey, our group operations officer, we were hoping to go into town, we told the sergeant. Would he like to accompany us? "No, thanks," the sergeant grinned, wrench in hand. "I've got a little more to do around here, but I'll see you later. Have a great time!" That was Koumarelos. He babied that plane like it was part of his own body. I really didn't believe there was a better all-around aircraft maintenance guy in the entire group. Our crew was lucky to have him.

Because of Connery and Mullins, a gunner named Farley, and my own claims to Irish ancestry (which Gus and Pat disparaged as the imaginings of an "Orangeman"), we had given Tally Koumarelos a name that tagged him as one of our crew and followed him throughout the war. We dubbed him "Kelly."

"Kelly" was twenty-nine or thirty, a little older than the four officers. I think Gus Connery was twenty-four or twenty-five, Pat Mullins, twenty-four, and Bob Russell must have been twenty-six or twenty-seven. Arthur (Pappy) Welch, our experienced radio operator, may have been the eldest of our crew at thirty-one. Hence, the nickname we'd given him. Gus was as agreeable and generally accommodating as an aircraft commander could be with any crew of ten. He wasn't an imposing figure. He must have been around five-eight, and weighed about 155 pounds. A quick wit and considerate nature made Gus easy to like, but there was something more. Gus Connery had unusually sound judgment, which made it impossible not to respect him.

When it came time to name, christen, and paint a distinctive logo on our own special airplane, we painted a big green shamrock on the fuselage, and the crew voted to name it, over Connery's vocal protest, *Gus's Bus*.

Hailing from New Providence, Rhode Island, a volunteer city fireman before joining the Air Corps, Connery didn't drink or smoke. He and Pat went to mass every Sunday. Gus never courted trouble of any kind. He wasn't a daredevil. He'd been an instructor pilot at Ellington Field in Houston, receiving his captain's bars there before coming to the 380th at Davis-Monthan.

Bob Russell, our copilot, was from Nashville, a commercial artist by trade. Somewhere, Bob had acquired a taste for light opera. He knew the words to all the operatic arias. Pat Mullins was from Somerville, Massachusetts, near Boston, and wanted to be an accountant. He and Gus had an Irish heritage and New England backgrounds in common while Bob and I were southerners, but we melded together like the fingers of a hand.

There had to be a healthy degree of camaraderie and a peculiar bonding between young fellows of disparate backgrounds and differing natures to make a successful aircrew. We had developed an easy, bantering repartee among us that bespoke acceptance of one another.

Once, as we laughed about the Aussies' reference to all of us as "Yanks," I asked Gus if he thought the dictionary defined a distinction between a "yank" and a "jerk." Picking up on the drift of my insult, Gus cheerfully replied, "The same difference as there is between a Tex and a Mex." Mullins quickly added, "Don't mind Jim, Gus. He's from down there where they don't know a Mick from a Spic." And we all had a good laugh, innocent of the demands of political correctness that one day would make such banter out of bounds.

Such was the relationship that would ripen from mutual respect into genuine, if unspoken, affection. "Kelly" Koumarelos was as much a part of this as were all of the four officers. One thing that distinguished the Air Corps from other branches of the service, I think, was a greater degree of informality and even an informal brotherhood between officers and enlisted personnel. This was especially true among the members of a bomb crew. Nobody "pulled rank," nor had to. There'd be times when it was us against the world.

So Kelly knew he was free and welcome to go with us that day in Hawaii, as he would do other times on relaxed social jaunts. If anything separated him from the rest of our crowd, it was his maturity and never-failing seriousness about things that were serious—such as the health of our airplane.

Bob Russell and I were particularly interested in seeing some native Hawaiians in their natural habitat. We wanted to soak up some local culture while we were there. None of us knew much about Hawaiians, except for Bing Crosby and Dorothy Lamour and popular songs like "Sweet Leilani" and "Blue Hawaii." Heading into town by bus, we passed a village of thatched huts and asked to be let off the bus so we might walk through its streets and visit, but we were told the native villages were off-limits to military personnel.

Since I'd learned to play the ukulele at about age ten, I'd always associated that instrument with Hawaii. I was eager, now, to hear some authentic Hawaiian ukulele music. An army guy on the inbound bus told us the name of a place where he said we could hear Hawaiian music, but told us it didn't open until about seven. So far, we had spotted a good many native Hawaiians. None of them bore much resemblance to Dorothy Lamour.

Meanwhile, we settled for a trip to Waikiki Beach, promising ourselves we'd try to get out to Pearl Harbor before leaving the island. The beach itself was achingly beautiful, but the few fine hotels were commandeered, we learned, by navy personnel. Off bounds to us Air Corps types. Hawaii seemed a mighty damn off-putting place, we laughed.

I had pulled a swimsuit out of my B-4 bag before leaving Hickam and insisted on taking a swim. I thought it would be great to say I'd been swimming at Waikiki. It was, for a swimmer, an enormous disappointment to discover for the first time how unforgiving a coral bottom can be to human feet. Nothing is the way you think it is going to be.

We found the bistro where native music alternated with mainland tunes. It was fun for a while and briefly diversionary. I asked the combo to play "Sweet Leilani." It was vaguely wistful. Then someone sang, "You must remember this, a kiss is still a kiss, a sigh is just a sigh . . ." After that, we left the lighted gardenlike room decorated with palm fronds, and stepped outside into the darkest night anyone would expect to see in the middle of a city full of people.

There were no identifying lights outside any building, not even streetlights. If there was much of a moon, it hid behind a cloud somewhere. Any automobiles moving in the streets drove without headlights. When the bus came, headed for Hickam, we saw its approach only by one faint pinpoint of light. No visible sign told us its destination. We had to ask the driver if he was going to Hickam Field.

We knew, for the first time, what the word "blackout" really meant.

# 10

## CROSSING THE WIDE PACIFIC

WE TOOK OFF FROM HICKAM FIELD early, bound for Christmas Island—just a tad east of due south and about seven hours distant, depending on what winds we encountered. Gus was anxious to arrive in the area well before midafternoon, while ample daylight remained.

The island was a small visual target in the vast blue Pacific, leaving little tolerance for even a minor navigational miscalculation, and we wanted every advantage our eyes could give us. But the main reason for our eagerness to get to Christmas Island early was rooted in a harrowing account we'd heard at Hickam. It involved members of our own group.

We'd learned that, just a few days earlier, the vanguard cadre of seven planes accompanying Col. Miller had encountered a highly dangerous situation upon arriving in the Christmas Island vicinity at late evening. Thunderstorms were thrashing the area, obscuring sight of land. Nobody on any of those seven B-24s could see any landing lights to mark the strip. Unsure of their own location vis-à-vis the runway, Col. Miller radioed the tower to ask airfield operators to activate a rotating beacon light so the pilots could see where the field lay.

Minutes passed. The B-24s circled, awaiting a light. No light appeared. Darkness was starting to fall. Despairing, the pilots began flying rectangular patterns, seeking visual contact with the ground. Some worried that they'd run out of fuel. Finally, one sighted the dim row of landing lights parallel to the runway, faintly winking through the downpour. All seven finally came in for safe landings, but the darkness, rain, and tension had made for a hair-raising experience.

Once on the ground, Col. Miller sought out the local airfield commander and registered a vigorous complaint that their pleas for a rotating beacon had been ignored. All seven of the crews were outraged, tired, and angry. The local commander replied that a Japanese submarine had been sighted offshore near the island that very afternoon. Had he turned on the beacon light, he feared, the sub crew could know exactly where to aim their guns for a direct hit on his outpost and landing strip.

With this encounter in mind, we'd made certain before taking off to tank up with more than enough fuel to last us for a loitering period before landing if bad weather or other contingencies should intervene. We'd also tested to make certain our fuel tanks had sprung no leaks during the fifteen-hour trip from San Francisco (as had happened to one plane in our loose entourage).

As we left the southernmost of the Hawaiian Islands behind, I reflected on the reported clash between our commander and the top ground officer at Christmas Island. I'd come to regard Colonel Miller as an eminently reasonable man. Never had I observed any evidence of ill temper. Quick to express approval, Miller had seemed slow to anger. At thirty-six and a former airline command pilot before joining the Air Corps, he was obviously steeped in flying experience. I instinctively identified with Miller's position—what chance does an aircrew have if it runs out of gas and can't see the ground?

Still, I had to suppose the ground commander at Christmas would be above summarily denying a landing beacon to lost aircrews without excellent cause. Though knowing little of a submarine's capability to wreak havoc with a ground installation, I'd heard of cases, just off the coasts of Florida and Texas, in which enemy subs had sunk large tankers and freighters while civilians on shore had watched, helpless to intervene.

It came to me that each of these two men had different, and overriding, responsibilities to the people under his own command. That's leadership. Though our armed forces were united by common purpose and interdependent in our national goals, there'd be times, I decided, when each of us would have to depend on himself and those closest to him. The six of us in that skeleton crew occupying *Gus's Bus* at that moment, I figured, shared the most critical of all identities of interest. Our first responsibility was survival.

ON COURSE OVER THE MID-PACIFIC, so deep and wide and definitively blue, I realized that after leaving the Hawaiian chain there lay great stretches with no islands in sight, anywhere. How could anyone steer a sure course to a land destination without a compass? I wondered about the Tahitians of several centuries ago who reportedly had realized their island was overpopulated and sent outriders in several directions to locate unpopulated lands they could colonize. Some of those exploratory crews in their longboats had discovered the Hawaiian chain, while others had ventured as far south on this ocean's billowing surface as New Zealand, several thousands of miles away, where snow falls. The point of my wonder was how they'd found their way without any of the navigational aids on which we now depended.

A navigation instructor at Williams Field had told me once, to my fascination, that the early Maoris and Hawaiians appeared to have mastered a now-lost navigational skill. They'd learned, he said, to discover the location of island masses far beyond their view by reading and studying the visual illusions that we call mirages, elusive refractions of reality that shimmer on heat waves at land or ocean level. Sailors, I would learn, call these "loomings."

Having traveled in summer through West Texas and New Mexico, I was familiar with the phenomenon. I'd often seen on hot, hazy days what looked like lakes or clumps of trees, and once, what looked like three office buildings teasing my eyes with their fake appearance of reality at some spot of barren prairie about a half-mile or so away from me. There are stories about people going crazy while chasing after false images of oases on the world's most arid deserts. The accepted theory has been that these things our eyes try to latch onto actually exist—somewhere else.

The early Tahitian sailors, according to my professor, had taught themselves to see the miragelike reflection of an island, nonexistent at the point of its apparition on the waters, and divine from the location of the sun and the clouds exactly where to find the reality—the very island whose glimmering image, reflected off a cloud surface, now taunted their vision. I'd discussed this theory with Pat, my current authority on things navigational. Trying it out in our minds one day, we concluded the ability to locate a distant island by this means, at sea level, must require a practiced skill that was as much art as science.

"It must be like billiards," I suggested, "trying to figure the exact point and angle at which to bounce the pool ball off the side board into a corner pocket." Pat agreed. "Or like holding a mirror in your hand to catch the sun, and moving it so you can put the blinding spot of sunlight in somebody's eye," he laughed. It was one of those mysteries we'd discuss from time to time and never really master. A couple of times when flying over a hazy ocean on a hot day we'd try to discover such a mirage reflected on the ocean's surface by clouds, but we gave it up, deciding finally that the arcane art, if it had existed at all, could be practiced only at ocean level, not from the sky.

Despite our shortcomings in ancient navigational esoterica, Pat's dead reckoning was right on the money that day. He'd figured the winds aright and vectored a true course. Gus's steady hand on the stick hadn't allowed our craft to waver even slightly from the path. Shortly after noon, the island's shape loomed on the horizon ahead, exactly on the nose. The weather was sparkling clear; we'd need no searchlight.

After taxiing to a station indicated by our jeepborne escort, we tied down the big bird and chocked the wheels, checked in at base operations, got two jeeps, and followed the ground officer's directions to a small cluster of tents with a great view of the beach just beyond a row of coconut palms. So this was Christmas Island!

"Must be the Waldorf Pacifica," said Bob Russell. "It's Christmas, but this can't be the North Pole," Gus bantered. "No igloos."

OUR FLIGHT PLAN the next morning named Nandi Field in the Fijis as our destination. It lay south-by-southwest, indicating a 205-degree heading. All of us were settling more comfortably into our tasks. We'd checked winds aloft. Our new drift meter was working, and I managed to find a few stationary objects below on which to focus for a reading of the winds. The successful flights to Oahu and Christmas fed our confidence.

These first two legs of our journey had yielded pleasant surprises. In Hawaii we'd discovered the distinctive flavor of fresh pineapple, right out of the fields, whose "eyes have never seen a can" as our radio operator Pappy Welch put it. On Christmas Island we learned the art of husking and splitting open a ripe coconut, fallen straight from a palm tree. In both cases, the flesh of the ripe, unprocessed native fruit is surprisingly crisper, more delicate in flavor, and in the case of the pineapple, less sour-sweet than the canned variety.

We'd seen the fabled gooney birds, awkwardly comic feathered creatures of these islands. They reminded us of student pilots, coming in too fast for a landing and almost nosing over. We amused ourselves for almost an hour watching them swoop down so clumsily for crumbs dropped on the beach. And our senses were tweaked by the wild orchids and frangipani that grew in such profusion. The vegetation was lush and green in the faintly salty air.

The islands themselves were deceptively entrancing as we flew over them. The voluptuous richness of the interior foliage, the whiteness of their wave-washed beaches, and the unexpected color of the coral reefs that jutted out beneath the water, so visible from the air, to frame the island's contours in varying hues of softer aqua-marine before surrendering finally to the ocean's dark and somber blue—these made it easy to forget momentarily that we'd come there to drop bombs and fight a war.

But this was our task. Our crew and the others in our squadron had been training together daily for four full months. Practicing, practicing. Each crew both a team in itself, and part of the larger team. Flying patterns; shooting at targets pulled through the air by drones until we could lead the moving targets just enough and pre-dictably hit them; making repetitive bomb runs, at different altitudes, each time dropping bombs on little white shacks surrounded by white concentric circles painted on the earth to mark the nearness of our misses. After all these years, I still remember the surge of satis-faction I felt the first time a bomb I'd dropped scored a direct hit.

That was just it. We took pride in one another's successes, and none of us ever wanted to disappoint the team. In the process, we'd learned enough about one another's jobs to relieve a teammate if needed. Throughout our training, we'd built a growing confidence in the *unit*, the crew that depended on us and on which we de-pended. At least that was the rationale, the ideal behind it, and it worked pretty well. Not perfectly, but better than some expected; and maybe better than we realized. We all had been getting better at what we did. And our confidence kept growing.

Things had not always gone smoothly. There'd been snags and glitches. Gus was not satisfied with the first aircraft engineer as-signed to us. Our crew commander had wanted someone on whom we could rely implicitly, someone with a vast knowledge and expe-rience with all the airplane's mechanisms. This plane, after all, was our home, our career, our very hold on life. That initial sergeant's knowledge seemed at times tentative, and his attitude hesitant. Medics one day told us that the man had tested positive for syphilis. Gus absolutely refused to take him, and the sergeant was returned to the unassigned pool for hospitalization, rehab, and reassignment.

That's when we found Kelly, a godsend. In retrospect, I've little doubt that we owe our survival at least partly to Tally Koumarelos.

Pappy Welch knew the radio inside and out. We'd have been in deep water at times—quite literally—if we'd suffered a radio failure that cut us off at a critical moment from flight formation teammates or the tower at home base. I believed, and so did Gus, that Pat Mullins was the best navigator in the squadron. As for Gus and Bob, they as well as the rest of us seemed ever mindful of the first equation we were taught in flight school: *There are old pilots, and there are bold pilots; but there are no old, bold pilots.*

Gus and his understudy, Bob, were personality opposites. Augustus V. Connery was gregarious; Robert Russell tended by nature to be a loner. Gus was a meat-and-potatoes guy, while Bob exhibited at times an epicurean palate. Where our top pilot was a teetotaler who neither smoked nor swore, Bob enjoyed leisurely savoring the aroma of a fine glass of wine with dinner, if one were available, and finishing with a Cuban after-dinner cigar. Our copilot most surely was the only one of our crew ever to have worn a set of tails to the opera, probably the only one of us ever to entertain any such aspiration.

Yet, with all our differences, we'd learned to have confidence in one another. Neither of our pilots had a wild hair when it came to flying the plane, or exhibited any temptation to stunt. Flying, with both, was strictly business. And Gus, by his demeanor and experience as an instructor pilot, inspired a quiet confidence.

One pilot of the 529th Squadron, Lieutenant Fred Hinze, sometimes had difficulty restraining his ebullience in the cockpit, to the sharp chagrin of Colonel Miller, who took a decidedly dim view of "buzzing." The B-24s, Miller insisted, weren't designed for flashy "on the deck" performances. On one overland training flight from Denver to southern California, Fred succumbed to the temptation to relieve his boredom by hugging the ground for most of the distance to see how many jackrabbits and coyotes he could stir up. The escapade drew a severe reprimand from the colonel as well as a threat of grounding.

Colonel Miller never fully tamed Fred Hinze. He was just one of those free spirits who tended to follow his own drummer. But we'd learn later on that there was a lot more to Lt. Fred Hinze than just a hot pilot with an irrepressible sense of derring-do. Fred was a man with a great big heart, as we'd see six months later. Still, no one could blame our group commander, back in March, for cracking down on all "stunt" flying.

We'd had two tragic accidents in the group during the crews' long weeks of training, and Miller held himself responsible for seeing that there'd be no more, short of actual combat. Both mishaps had come in February while we were flying out of Biggs Field in El Paso.

Other rough spots of one kind or another had cropped up during our training, but no other casualties. Now here we were, crossing the Pacific, crew by crew, to test our hard-won skills. Our next stop would be Fiji.

# II

## DAYDREAMS AND REALITIES

AT AGE FIFTEEN I'd fantasized about one day flying over the Pacific and finding Amelia Earhart, the American aviatrix who, in the summer of 1937, had disappeared without trace somewhere in this ocean's vastness. In one such Walter Mitty-like adolescent daydream, she had become a missionary, teaching and helping the native population. In another version, by the time I'd found her, she'd grown much prettier and become a sex goddess, ruling a Polynesian tribe. At fifteen, like a lot of American boys, I'd had a hard time deciding just which goddess to pursue.

That was the start of my junior year in high school, the year I banged up my knee early in the football season. A chipped cartilage swelled the knee to the size of a small watermelon. That mishap required lancing, bandaging, and six weeks on crutches, which knocked me out of play for the rest of the season. At that point, my ambition had been to become a football coach. Coaches Bob Harris and Pop Noah were my role models. Now Coach Harris, seeing I was sidelined for that fall, recruited me for the school's debate team, insisting the competitive value of a top debater was easily equal to that of a top halfback.

Harris taught our World History class, and in the process of trying to impress him, I'd begun studying history like a fiend and gotten hooked on the subject. It was fall, 1937. Hitler was invading the Sudetenland, then Czechoslovakia. Mussolini's troops were in Ethiopia, and the Japanese army was running rampant in China. When our history course arrived at the World War I period the next spring, I developed the conviction that Woodrow Wilson had been right. The U.S. Senate turned aside our chances for peace when it refused to ratify the Versailles Treaty and U.S. membership in the League of Nations. Another, bigger world war seemed to be inching ever closer. It was then I had decided that, even better than coaching football, I'd prepare myself and go to Congress one day, there to work for peace and straighten all this out. It was a heady dream and it lasted me into my third year of college.

Well, that was then and this was now. At the moment, we were in the real world. Flying a real airplane over the real Pacific to fight a real war. Against a real enemy.

ON FIJI WE DISCOVERED a native population distinctly different from the Polynesians of the mid-Pacific. These were more willowy, rangy people with fuzzier hair and darker skin. While there, we were invited to witness a tribal or cultural ceremony, in which several younger men were being inducted into some type of society, at one point expected to drink a potion of indeterminate dark gray liquid, which smelled faintly like turpentine, and was passed around in a communal vessel that looked like a skull.

I never fathomed the nature of this ritual or the reason for our seeing it, but the whole context of what we observed while at Nandi told me that the Fiji Islanders were solidly on our side in the struggle with Japan, and willing hosts to our military personnel. Some tall members of the community, a few in khaki uniforms and others armed with long spears, proudly stood guard over our parked aircraft. When I inquired about this, I was told by U.S. military people on the ground that working for—and receiving what to us would be very nominal wages from—the American armed forces was considered a prestigious occupation of the highest order among the Fiji peoples.

Copilot Bob Russell, ever the artist, took time to make some sketches on a pad he'd brought with him. During the couple of days at Hickam Field, Bob had often been recruited to help other crews paint distinctive nose art on their assigned B-24s. The planes were otherwise tinted with varying shades of dark and dusty green in camouflage patterns, intended to confound and conceal the distinctive aircraft shape so that they might blend into their surroundings. In the military world of general uniformity and often boring regimentation, the startling individuality of our aircraft nose art was a refreshing exercise in imaginative freedom of expression.

Among our group, the names and artistic displays with which different crews chose to adorn their bombers ranged from a B-24 named *Prince Valiant,* which bore a picture of a knight in armor, to one dubbed *The Red Ass,* portrayed by a bright red donkey with a wicked, aggressive look on its face. Popular themes sometimes embraced pictures of scantily clad girls, their idealized shapes often reflecting the influence of popular *Esquire* magazine artists Petty and Vargas. *Miss Giving,* decorating the B-24 by that name, was depicted as a curvaceous blond in a short negligee and high heels, kneeling and smiling graciously, with her right arm raised high while the fingers of the hand toy with a bomb that looks ready to drop. Another, dubbed *She 'Asta,* showed a leggy nude brunette reclining on her back with her right knee lifted and the toe pointing earthward. Then, there was the bomber named *Deliverer,* represented by a white stork in flight carrying from its beak what looked like a long diaper—with a bomb, instead of a baby, nestled in its folds. On the plane named *Alley Oop,* someone had painted a picture of the comic-strip caveman about to throw a bomb he held in his right hand like a football.

Russell, more than the rest of us, seemed to be getting into the spirit of the islands. He'd begun growing a neat, pencil-thin mustache like that of actor Adolphe Menjou, and a trim goatee which in time would come to a fine point beneath the tip of his chin. The rest of us laughingly accused him of copying the French painters like Gauguin, preparing to paint famous canvases of South Sea island life. Bob just grinned slyly.

"When in Rome, my lads," he said.

"When in Rome, what?" someone demanded.

"When in Rome, don't write graffiti on the ceiling of the Sistine Chapel," Bob responded.

AT THE OFFICERS' CLUB on New Caledonia, we ran into some B-17 and B-25 flight crewmen who had participated personally just a few weeks earlier in the Battle of the Bismarck Sea. This had been one of the two most decisive battles of the Pacific War, an enormous victory for U.S. airpower. The news of that impressive triumph had been a big morale builder while we were training at Denver, before we knew we'd be coming to the Pacific. Now, it was doubly exciting to realize that these very guys who'd accepted our invitation to pull their table over to join ours had been part of that action.

They were willing to talk, and we were anxious to listen. We plied them with more questions than a radio quiz show. Through two rounds of beer, they indulged our curiosity and, surprising to us, seemed almost as hungry to hear news fresh from stateside as we to soak up their story. But mainly this was their night to talk.

Their firsthand accounts of that classic struggle in the Bismarck Sea, which lies between New Guinea and New Britain, were mesmerizing. The epic encounter had begun as a Japanese initiative. Admiral Yamamoto and his command staff were eager to drive U.S. and Australian forces completely off New Guinea where we then held a tenuous foothold.

With a massive convoy of eight destroyers and eight transport ships filled with more than 6,000 assault troops, our foes set out from their base at Rabaul, New Britain, bound for Lae on the New Guinea coastline. The Japanese armada moved stealthily beneath and behind a massive cloud system, our new friends explained, plotting to avoid early detection by Allied forces. But an Australian reconnaissance crew flying a U.S. Liberator bomber sighted the movement before it reached halfway across the Bismarck Sea.

Alerted, our 43rd and 90th Bomb Groups first sent a wave of B-17s, which sank two of the destroyers. As the other ships of the invading force steamed ahead, our 5th Air Force had a field day. With help from Australian crews, our B-24, B-25 and B-17 bombers blew up four of the eight destroyers and sent all eight enemy troop transports to the bottom. U.S. and Aussie fighters strafed the slowly sinking ships and flotsam repeatedly with machine-gun fire. In all, the Allied strike stranded, gunned, and drowned at least 3,000 troops of the invading Japanese army. "Japs were everywhere you looked in the water," said one of the four, "hundreds, hundreds of them, trying to hang onto some piece of the ships, anything. God, it was like a gunnery range."

The two big surprises seemed to be, according to these participants, that for once we'd been wily enough to outwit our enemy in using the weather to our advantage, and further, that our guys had very nearly perfected the art of skip-bombing. The most devastating bomb run came as about eighty U.S. long- and medium-range bombers flew straight out of the west just before sundown with the sun's bright glare directly behind them. They came low, just above mast level, barely high enough to clear the ships' infrastructure.

Our informants were eager to spill out their story to someone who hadn't been there to see it. Many of our bombs, released close-up, split into the vessels' hulls. Our fighters, too, had shot down as many as seventy-five Japanese aircraft, one of the four surmised. Estimates of total Japanese casualties ran from 3,000 to 12,000. It was hard to pinpoint, but the day's work had destroyed the equivalent of an entire Japanese division.

One of the fellows was a bombardier named Jake—or something. His teammates kept calling him by a nickname, "Daredevil." I soon deemed the moniker appropriate when Daredevil began describing to me, as a fellow bombardier, the raptures of skip-bombing a Japanese ship.

"You haven't had such a thrill since you were a kid and rode a 'Loop-the-Loop' at the state fair for the first time!" Daredevil exclaimed excitedly. "You're comin' right at 'em like a bat outta hell; you're sittin' right there in the nose cone wonderin' if your feet are gonna get wet, you're flyin' so low, you got your finger just light on the toggle switch, and you're not gonna toggle the bombs 'til you're close enough to see the shape of a person, and then—and then, ya let go! BLAM! And 'til that moment, ya don't know if it's gonna be the Fourth of July or Easter Sunday mornin' in church!"

I tried not to shudder outwardly at the implication of that last metaphorical choice. It occurred to me that Daredevil had rehearsed this story before, but that took nothing away from the vividness and fervor of this recitation. I supposed that he relived the thrill with each retelling.

We and our newfound colleagues soon were signing one another's "short snorter" bills. This was a popular Air Corps fad. Currency of any country or denomination would do. When one bill was filled with signatures of other flyboys, it was common to attach it to another, and then a third, by Scotch tape or other adhesive. The autographed bills, thus stuck together end-to-end, were then rolled tightly. Some fellows wound up with a roll almost too rotund to fit inside a trouser pocket, made up of currencies from as many nations as they'd visited. As I write this, I wonder whatever happened to all those treasures. I haven't seen a "short snorter" bill in fifty years.

After all of us took leave of the officers' club that evening, I began to ponder whether low-level bombing would assume a larger than expected role in our combat missions. Our crew had not practiced it. As the bombardier, I'd scarcely even tried it. Our whole training regimen had been built around the Norden bombsight. Supposedly the world's most advanced bombing instrument, the Norden was an early harbinger of the computer age, almost a half-century yet in the future. It required some fairly sophisticated calculations that had taken me months to master, and a certain manual dexterity, but it provided the edge that let us dare label what we did as "precision" bombing. Although it was the envy of every other nation (or so we'd been told), the Norden, I figured, would be absolutely useless in skip-bombing.

One other thought kept nagging at me. Two of the fellows had apparently *enjoyed* the plight of the drowning Japanese. They told of it with such relish! I wondered if all combat forces, after sustained or repeated hostile contact, developed personal feelings of hatred or loathing toward their enemies. An unavoidable reaction, maybe. It's them or us, after all. Those 3,000 highly armed Japanese who went to their watery deaths in the Bismarck Sea had been on their way to invade the camps of our own troops on New Guinea. They were out to kill us, and killing is what war is about. I had crossed that bridge when I volunteered for combat flying. Okay, so let it lie. I willed myself to go to sleep.

FROM NEW CALEDONIA, we embarked for Brisbane on the fifth and final leg of our journey. When finally our wheels touched the runway at Amberley Field, we figured that our gentle, semicircular route to the east and south of Japanese-held territory had covered close to nine thousand flight miles. We'd logged just about forty-six hours of actual flying, and the journey had taken us eight days. None of us, then, would have thought there'd ever come a time when passengers could book a nonstop commercial flight from San Francisco to Sidney and arrive in just fourteen hours. But, of course, that time is here.

# 12

## NEW HOME IN THE OUTBACK, DOWN UNDER

I LIKED THE AUSSIES. Maybe that's because they seemed to like us. Their country and ours, after all, had sprung from the same tree. It was easy to forget that ours, like theirs, had once been used as a British penal colony. Or, maybe I identified with the Aussies because they seemed so much like Texans with a funny accent. They were a friendly, open, and hospitable folk; sometimes tough, proud, and fiercely independent, without airs or affectations, plainly down to earth and genuine.

The Aussie men I came to know in their armed services were enjoyable, sometimes rowdy companions. Not many months earlier, when the Japanese had controlled almost all of New Guinea and before our ground forces established and held onto a firm beachhead at the south of that island, the Japanese sent bombing raids over eastern Australian cities. A favorite target was Townsville, where General MacArthur had established U.S. Army headquarters after being driven from the Philippines. Aussie pilots, lacking the sophisticated interceptor planes so badly needed in the defense of Britain, had mounted a gallant if brash defense of their cities, flying antiquated Tiger Moth trainer planes, inexpertly equipped with machine guns and whatever other weapon they could put their hands on.

In Brisbane, Charters Towers, and Townsville, I thought I could imagine myself in Texas a generation earlier. Australia was almost exactly as big geographically as the United States in those years before the addition of Alaska. But when we arrived there, in 1943, it was peopled by only about six million, roughly the same number then living in Texas.

In Townsville, we awaited enstationment orders from the 5th Air Force, to which we now belonged. Thirty-five of the 380th's crews had made it. One was lost, somewhere in the vast Pacific, not heard from since the morning of April 26 when it took off from Hawaii. For two weeks we'd held out hope of some message. None came. Whether downed by mechanical failure or navigational error, or whether any survived, we'd never know. Two of the crewmen were friends of mine. Clarence (Con) Corpening, pilot, and Everett (Rocky) Stoner, bombardier, and my classmate at Williams Field, stuck in my mind. Today, more than sixty years later, I can close my eyes, see their faces. Their voices resonate in my ear. Some of the things we talked about revisit me. Also aboard was copilot Richard St. Dennis, married two days earlier at Hamilton Field. Their fate, like that of Amelia Earhart, remains a mystery of the mid-Pacific and its hauntingly beautiful islands.

From some American ground troops in the Townsville vicinity, we'd hear disparaging remarks about the Allied headquarters building, built partly as an underground bunker and fortified heavily with steel and concrete. Critics seemed to see it as an ego trip of some sort for General MacArthur. Our supreme commander's popular nickname, among sundry troops below field-grade rank, was "Dugout Doug." I never really got the hang of their complaints. From my point of view, the fortifications MacArthur built there were no more than practical necessities warranted by the war.

Second-guessing the generals was one of the idle exercises with which junior officers often filled vacuums of time and moments of boredom while awaiting military action. To the best of my knowledge, there wasn't a West Pointer in the entire 380th. But if we had at best a worm's-eye view of tactics, we tended to think our bird's-eye view of targets qualified us to express opinions on the folks who were running the war. Eisenhower seemed to be generally popular, and none of our guys had a bad word for Hap Arnold. But you could buy an argument on George Patton in half the time it took you to salute. His partisans and critics were equally vocal. And a lot of those eager for something to pontificate about seemed to have the opinion that MacArthur ought to be up there in New Guinea right now leading a counteroffensive to push the Japanese off into the Coral Sea.

I never heard this complaint—or for that matter, any other criticism of American forces—from the Aussies. They could be quite profane in their assessment of Australia's own military or political leaders, but we were their guests, and, for the most part, heartily welcome. The only friction of which I was ever aware involved a probably natural resentment among young Australian men toward their better-paid American counterparts, suddenly turned loose in such numbers in their country. Many thousands of Australia's young men were fighting the war abroad and suffering heavy casualties in places like North Africa, while their own homeland was practically overrun by hordes of U.S. servicemen with comparatively a lot of money to spend on the Australian girls they'd been forced to leave behind. Or so the story went. And I could see some logic to it.

We finally learned from the 5th Air Force Command that a whole new base was being built especially for our group's occupancy in the Northern Australian outback. As we transferred within a few weeks to that location, the men of the 380th were thrown into direct contact with Australians in a combat setting. We sensed no rivalry. We were on the same team.

The 5th Air Force, in fact, attached us for administrative purposes to the Australian Defense Command, and that was an arrangement unique, we would learn, to our particular bomb group. Technically, we were part of the Royal Australian Air Force (RAAF). Several Australian air crewmen were assigned to our group, and more would be. Our commander, Col. Miller, reported to Australian Air Vice Marshal (AVM) Adrian Cole. Our troops began referring to him, more affectionately than derisively, as "King" Cole. He reported, in turn, to General Kenney.

FLYING OVER THE VAST REACHES of Australia's underpopulated Northern Territory was like seeing stretches of Arizona, Utah, and West Texas strung together beneath us. Darwin, the North's one real city, had been evacuated of civilians months earlier when a Japanese invasion seemed likely. The land was mostly plains, punctuated by a few hills and a couple of stingy rivers, that briefly swelled and widened in the rainy season, and pocked in places with huge anthills. Where grass grew, it was mostly sun-parched and yellowed by late May. "Down under," there in the Southern Hemisphere, we figured the month of May was equivalent to late November at home. Still, it showed no signs of turning cooler there in Australia's vast north country.

No longer while flying at night could we get our bearings from the North Star or even see the Big Dipper. For stellar directional guidance we had to find the Belt of Orion, or the Southern Cross, which isn't visible in skies above the United States.

In daytime, herds of kangaroos and their smaller cousins, the wallabies, could be seen crossing the plains. There were big birds called emus, remindful of the ostrich family. Occasionally, here or there, someone on a flying crew would spot a patch of dingoes, feral dogs descended from work animals that had accompanied the earliest white settlers of the inhospitable outback. Yellowish and with upward-pointed ears, these dogs now ran in packs like American coyotes, stalking whatever game seemed vulnerable.

It was maybe just a bit over 90 miles by air, and almost 120 by road, from Darwin south to the remote location of Fenton Airstrip. The road was made of hard clay and unpaved, with washboard ridges chiseled out by the rough-riding lorries that the Aussies drove.

Between Fenton Strip and Darwin on this little-used highway lay a settlement called Adelaide River. It had five or six stores, buildings with corrugated-tin roofs, and looked like a remnant of the old American West. Its name was taken from the sparse watercourse on whose banks the settlement was built in this arid country. There had been several early efforts, in fact, at gold mining in that vast northern stretch of land, and occasional relics of those days could be found by a determined explorer.

There were widely scattered farms and ranches (called "stations" in Australian parlance). Those that survived were huge. It took a lot of acreage to wrestle out a living from this inhospitable land. But on those occasions when a jeepload of U.S. soldiers or airmen descended on a ranch house with its broad veranda, we were invariably greeted with open arms and a hearty invitation to come in and share dinner. Or at least a pot of tea.

People on the range were hungry for news of any kind. Usually they'd be happy to swap you a quarter of range-fed beef or some side meat from a hog they'd slaughtered for any old magazines we might find lying around the tent at Fenton. For labor, with so many Aussies mobilized in defense work, ranchers depended on families or tribes of Aborigines, the dark native wanderers of these rolling plains that had been their home long centuries before the coming of the white settlers.

Our advance contingent of the 380th arrived at Fenton in mid- to late May. Aussie construction crews had finished the broad airstrip, with thirty-five revetments, semicircular patches of paving sticking out from four paved lanes that connected with the main runway. Each revetment was surrounded by huge protective mounds of earth. Their purpose, obviously, was to guard the parked planes from shrapnel or incendiary projectiles likely to come in a bombing attack. The revetments were probably also useful in reducing the stress on the aircraft from the heavy winds that swept across the plains in certain seasons.

The construction crews had built a group headquarters, quartermaster depot, kitchen and mess hall facilities, fuel storage tanks for servicing the planes, trucks, and jeeps, latrines with underground septic tanks, and a storage tower from which water was piped to the buildings and the shower stalls.

I was told that the well diggers had engaged the services of an ancient Aborigine to "witch" the well site. Whatever the truth of that story, they'd found underground water there in the barren outback. We always had an abundance for both showers and any other necessary purposes. Our boast was "Hot and cold running water—depending on the time of day." In the early mornings, water from the showers ran almost icy cold and bracing. By early afternoon, following a half-day of strong sunlight on the water tower, the pipes gave forth a torrid flow fit for a Turkish harem.

The Aussies had done, in my estimation, a darn good job. The tough macadam substance of the runway and connecting arms was durable and resistant to both the weight of our planes and the fickle vagaries of the weather. (I would visit Fenton again in 1987, after it had been deserted for more than forty years, and find the runway superstructure still in usable condition. There must have been some iron ore mixed in with the sand and cement, for it had resisted the encroachments of rain, sun, wind, the desert grass, and the abrasive sand.)

When we arrived, the Aussie construction units were putting the finishing touches on one satellite living area reached by a dirt road from headquarters, and that's where the 530th was assigned. The 528th would share the buildings and amenities at group headquarters and pitch its permanent tents there. Each of the other squadrons had their own separate location. The 529th and the 531st were billeted at a place about eighty miles south called Manbulloo, on the crocodile-infested Katherine River. It had its own airstrip.

Our 530th squadron area was about a mile down the road from the Fenton landing strip. We had a squadron headquarters shack, a kitchen and mess hall, latrines and showers. We would live four men to a tent. Tents were assigned by quartermaster. It was up to us to cut the trees and erect our own dwelling. Then, we dug slit trenches nearby our living quarters into which we could dive for protection when Japanese air raids came.

# 13

## BAPTISM OF FIRE

IT MADE SENSE THAT the Koepang military cluster on Timor Island should be our first target. We had good reasons, personal as well as strategic, for wanting to put that most forward Japanese military breastworks, on the southwest corner of the island of Timor, out of commission. On the western edge of a jutting peninsula, at Koepang, was an active Japanese airdrome manned with bombers and fighters, while a well-equipped naval base, called Penfoel, covered the eastern side.

Short weeks earlier, when the 380th ground forces arrived from stateside by ship at Darwin harbor, they were greeted by a swarm of Japanese Zeros. The planes, flaunting the round red symbol of the rising sun on their fuselage, sprayed the ship and dock areas with 30-caliber bullets in repeated strafing passes and lobbed incendiary projectiles at the Australian lorries sent to pick up the ground personnel and their luggage. It had been a frantic, rude awakening for our group's ground support forces. Aussie pilots in Spitfires rose to engage the enemy in aerial combat, chasing them back across the Timor Sea after dropping two of the Zeros, burning, in the water.

The next night, back at base after their movement over the dusty road from Darwin to Fenton, some had listened by shortwave radio to a Japanese newscast beamed nightly to Allied listeners. That evening, the sweet, unctuous voice of the female propagandist welcomed the 380th Heavy Bomb Group by name to the South Pacific. The feminine newscaster, in surprisingly good English, reported the bold raid on Darwin, flamboyantly exaggerating the damage done, and ended with what we were told was her customary sign-off: "Tune in this same time tomorrow night—if you are still alive." The Japanese clearly wanted us to know that they knew who and where we were.

A few nights later, our base at Fenton was bombed for the first time. From an altitude that looked to me like about 12,000 feet, a late afternoon formation of Japanese bombers dropped explosives and incendiaries, disabling one of our aircraft and causing other property damage in the vicinity of the airfield.

Our intelligence people surmised that the bombers, as well as the fighters at the Darwin welcoming party, could have come only from Koepang, the base on Timor. Looking up the business end of their gun barrels as we were, it gave us every incentive we needed to destroy their nest.

The northern third of Australia was closely ringed in mid-1943 by Japanese occupation forces, entrenched on surrounding island chains. They formed a broad semicircle from the Solomon Islands in the east Coral Sea to western New Guinea in the north, and to Jakarta and Bandung on the Java Straits to the west. But the southern coast of Timor to our immediate northwest offered the closest and most immediate menace to ours and any other Allied targets in the northern territory.

Group Commander Miller explained the purpose of our mission to the flight crews assembled in our newly constructed 380th headquarters conference room on the night of June 10. He rolled out a large map of the Coral Sea, showing our route of flight.

Trying to calibrate distance on the map, I figured the enemy base that had already shown us its teeth was about as far from Fenton as Santa Fe from Fort Worth, or maybe Cleveland from

Philadelphia or Seattle from San Francisco. Col. Miller, a former senior pilot with American Airlines, would have had a more precise comparison, but nobody asked. This was our first group mission briefing. Mostly we listened.

We saw aerial photographs and drawings of the rather extensive Japanese military works—Koepang and Penfoel—clustered on the seaward corner of Timor. Miller assigned our squadrons three different targets. Ours was the airdrome, where we hoped to catch bombers on the ground. Others were assigned the port, in hopes of destroying shipping facilities and maybe vessels, and locations where we thought they stored their fuel.

Very early the next morning, June 11, we ate breakfast in the dark. Crews were all in position in our respective planes, the aircraft fueled and engines revved up, ready for takeoff by sunrise. We began taking off shortly after first good light. The whole group would be airborne by 7 A.M., and over the target in about an hour. The weather was good and visibility near perfect as we crossed the northern Australian coastline west of Darwin. I had studied the map and the photos carefully and knew what to look for. I'd cranked all the pertinent data into my Norden bombsight.

Precision bombing, we knew, depended on accurate data as well as manual dexterity on the part of the bombardier. On the last leg of a bomb run, the bombsight was actually guiding the plane on a pass designed to put the bombs exactly on target. The secret lay in calculating at what precise point in space to release the bombs from our given altitude.

It was a far cry from modern aerial destruction. Now a one- or two-man crew can put a missile on a laser beam and guide it inertially right onto the target as it speeds down its foreordained path. If we'd had this kind of equipment in those days, there'd have been no need for bombardiers.

Still, we'd been assured that our sophisticated Norden bombsight was the world's best and most accurate. So jealous were we of its falling into enemy hands that bombardiers were sworn, at likelihood of hostile forces taking possession of the aircraft, to destroy the delicate inner mechanisms of the Norden by deliberately firing into it two shots from the 45-caliber pistols we carried.

It was my job to justify this mission by seeing to it that our bombs landed on target. Several things were involved in the calculation. We might call them drift, draft, and drag. Since crosswinds could blow not only aircraft but also any foreign projectile off its intended course, the plane had to be flying a route just enough upwind of the target to compensate for drift on the bomb's downward journey.

And since any falling object descends at 32 feet per second/per second (meaning its earthbound speed increases to 64 feet in the second and to 96 feet in the third second, and so on), the precise ideal moment of release is governed by the exact height of the plane above the target as well as its lateral distance from a point directly above target.

But there's still another variable—the thing called "drag." At the moment a projectile leaves the plane, it is moving in exactly the same direction and speed as the aircraft. But, once out on its own, it is subject to slowing down and falling slightly behind. Just how much atmospheric drag affects the movement of a specific object varies according to the object's size and shape. Different bombs had different "ballistic coefficients." I had cranked into the Norden's mechanical brain the specific coefficient of the 500-pound models we were carrying that day.

Going over this data in my mind to be sure I had everything exactly right, and clocking our altitude above target at 9,200 feet, as I now recall, I watched the island of Timor as we closed distance on it. Then, there it was. I saw the port inlet to the right, and—up ahead, there—the landing strip!

We were on our bomb run . . . I looked through the sight, lined it up on the middle of the runway ahead, and began carefully applying the fingers of both hands, one on each of two knobs to the right and to the left of the instrument. I was lining the crosshairs directly on the desired impact spot for the middle bomb in our string of twelve . . . easy now, easy. Lower the horizontal hair ever so slightly. There, now. Hold it. Hold it right there. Hold it . . . .

Behind my station, in the nose of the plane, behind the pilots, radio operator, and top gunner, in the middle of the fuselage, the bomb bay doors had opened just as we began the bomb run, which could take thirty or forty seconds, or . . . .

"Bombs away," wing gunner Johnny Tackett reported over the intercom. I felt the torque of the plane rolling off to the left as Gus, reclaiming control of the aircraft, maneuvered a swift evasive action to get us out of the line of fire. I looked out front through the nose window.

Puffs of white smoke were exploding below us, maybe 300 feet low and off to the right. I hoped I'd been more accurate with my bombs than that Japanese anti-aircraft gunner with his shot. Now, just get out of the target area. Get out fast and head home. "We got lucky this time," I thought. My heart was racing.

Suddenly, through my headset, "Heads up! Three o'clock high!" And I spotted the Zeros, two at our altitude, coming at us fast from our right. My hands on the 50-caliber nose guns, I moved in their direction, but their rate of closure was too fast. They'd passed over us before I could get off a shot. But our top turret gunner had been firing, as well as our left wing gunner, as the Zeros were going away. We'd missed them both.

Soon we were joined by two other B-24s from our squadron, one on each wing. It was the three-plane formation in which we hoped to return to safety beyond the range of the Japanese fighter planes. If we can just make it for fifteen minutes, I calculated, that's seventy miles, and we'll run them out of gas.

A pack of six Zeros swarmed past us from the rear, firing. They turned and made two more passes at our three-plane formation. I could see the trajectory of their bullets. I got off one burst as they passed. It was hard to get good aim from the nose position. They were approaching from the rear and moving across our path alternately high and low to the sides, their guns spitting bullets.

Then we saw it. There was smoke, and the B-24 to my left began to lose altitude, a left prop feathered. The pilot had shut off the flow of fuel to the flaming engine to minimize the likelihood of explosion. I recognized it as the plane flown by a newly assigned pilot whom Gus had known back at Ellington Field. We lost altitude voluntarily, trying to follow our companion ship down for its protection, trying to stay close. Gus was talking on the intercom, explaining his intentions.

But the stricken plane was descending too fast, turning in the direction of the feathered propeller. It finally settled on the ocean. Two yellow life rafts popped out of the plane. We turned to see if the crew was making it to the life rafts. Then two Japanese planes passed in swift succession directly over the life rafts, firing their guns. We could see the splashes the bullets made on the ocean all around the rafts.

Now we'd descended to maybe 4,000 feet and were alone. Our homebound bomber formation was moving ahead of us, toward Darwin.

There was nothing we could do but pour on the coal and try to catch up. We couldn't help the downed crew. Maybe, we hoped . . . . I said a silent prayer. But the fate of that crew now was in the hands of God.

The stunning cruelty of the episode I'd just witnessed made its mark. Never before had I watched an act of such wanton bloodthirstiness as strafing helpless men in the water and riddling their life rafts with machine-gun fire. Yet, what had I expected? This was war. There was no room in the mind of the enemy for gallantry, noblesse oblige, or any of those knightly virtues that coaches and preachers talked about in high school and college. In the conduct of war there were no Marquis of Queensbury rules, no penalties for "unnecessary roughness."

This piece of action was particularly hard on Gus. The pilot of the downed plane had been his flying pupil back at Ellington Field. Gus surely wanted to help, as did we all. But his first responsibility was to the safety of his own crew. This, too, was war.

Suddenly, I realized that my hands were trembling. That was something new. I'd been calm as any steely-eyed gunslinger in the midst of the action. My hands on the bombsight, and later on the nose gun, had been steady as those of a card shark. Now that the action was over and the enemy left behind, I guess my nervous system belatedly recognized what we'd been through. It was the same way with others, I learned. It would be that way again. On other missions and in other crises—but only after the crisis had passed. Strange, but that's the way we're put together.

That afternoon, as we waited in the intelligence shack to be debriefed, I learned that eight of the twelve bombs from our plane had landed right on target, exploding on the runway where Japanese bombers were tied down. But the last three had trailed off apparently into the jungle at the runway's eastern end. Paul Stansbury, bombardier in the plane following us on the bomb run, had seen them. I'd released the string just a fraction of a second late. Still, eight out of twelve wasn't bad.

We'd done substantial damage to Japan's forward base that day. Other observers reported fires in the vicinity of the fuel storage unit. Still others reported that we'd busted up docking facilities at the port. I couldn't stop thinking about the fallen crew. Wondering if there was any way they might have gotten out, made it to shore? Probably not. The 531st, we'd learn, lost two ships that day, one piloted by that squadron's commanding officer, Captain James Dienelt, the other by Captain Paul Smith, its operations officer and second in command.

Our exhaustion was more emotional than physical. The squadron medic, a Captain Garron, told us we needed to get out on the volleyball court and get some physical exercise before we bunked down. Most of the guys rewarded this suggestion with a ribald response. They thought he was joking. Turns out he wasn't.

We were new at this, and now we were veterans. We'd dodged some real bullets. We felt sad about the crews we'd almost surely lost. We sure as hell didn't feel like playing volleyball.

We would learn, crazy as it seemed, that physical exercise is the best antidote after a mission. That lesson had come from RAF fly-ers in the Battle of Britain. The medical officer's well-intentioned advice that day got the raspberries and went totally unheeded. We still had things to learn.

# 14

## HAVE BOMBS, WILL TRAVEL

THROUGH THE SUMMER and fall of '43, the 380th was the only U.S. force capable of striking major Japanese installations in the Southwest Pacific. Other forces, from bases to our east, could pound and harass Japanese positions in the Solomons and upper New Guinea. But the range of our B-24 Liberators, at that time the longest-range bombers America had, gave us full responsibility for that wide sweep of formerly Dutch- and Portuguese-held territory that would become, at war's end, the Republic of Indonesia with the world's fourth-largest population.

As always in any military operation, rumors abounded. Some even turned out to be rooted in truth. Try as it might to quash the repetition of idle gossip and verbal speculation (billboards on state-side training bases warned us all that "Loose Lips Sink Ships"), military officialdom had an uphill battle. Back in February with the assignment to our group of an intelligence officer named Lt. Simaika, fluent in Arabic and steeped in the cultural lore of the Mideast, many of us had deduced that we were headed for North Africa. When we learned, to our belated surprise, that we were slated for Australian duty, our internal rumor mill concocted the supposition that a high-level appeal at the last minute had altered our course and rearranged our collective destiny. Many years later, it would be officially confirmed. Lieutenant General George C. Kenney, Commander of the 5th Air Force, had successfully pleaded with President Franklin D. Roosevelt in the early spring of 1943, for attachment of our B-24 group of long-range bombers to his command.

Now, through June and July of 1943, we kept hoping for an Allied breakthrough in the fortunes of our war against Japan. The Japanese forward momentum so indomitably relentless throughout 1942, had stalled with the Battle of the Bismarck Sea. But our enemies held on tenaciously to their forward positions. Our raids were bound to be weakening their positions, but we had little way of cataloging how much impact we were making on Japan's ability to continue the war.

WE FOUND OURSELVES bombing widely scattered targets. Few of our missions were flown in group strength. Most were squadron-size, with six to nine planes and crews participating. Even three- and four-plane missions were not uncommon. Twice our crew flew alone, assigned to reconnoiter and seek "targets of opportunity" in western New Guinea. Sometime around the end of July, a few of us, reviewing the scattered range of our group's bombing soirees with Squadron Intelligence Officer Ralph Oman, were amazed at the scope and range of the group's combined efforts. We began sticking pins in a big wall map to represent locations hit. We figured that maybe in the six weeks since our first full-scale assault on Timor, we'd collectively flown about 160 "sorties," meaning that many individual bomb runs over enemy targets.

Somebody said that might seem like small pickins' to the 8th Air Force crews flying in hundred-plane missions every day over Europe. The two wars weren't even comparable for anyone trying to quantify volumes of destruction. Unlike bomb crews flying out of England, we had no fighter escorts to help us deal with enemy interceptors. But that disadvantage was amply offset by German anti-aircraft gunners. Practiced in night-after-night raids, they had developed a diabolical accuracy that most of their inexperienced Japanese counterparts couldn't begin to match. There were a few known exceptions in our theater—Rabaul Harbor, notorious for its deadly "ack-ack," was one.

"Look at it this way," Intelligence Officer Oman suggested cheerfully, "we're learning more *geography* than they are in the Eighth Air Force."

Ralph Oman was a lawyer from Topeka, Kansas. I guess he must have been in his early forties. He had a quick sense of humor and a good tenor voice for harmonizing on the old songs, as some of us occasionally did in relaxed off-moments. Once one of our crews, on a reconnaissance sortie, dropped bombs on a village named Sorong on New Guinea's northern coast. We were unexpectedly chastised by some upper-echelon source. It seems that Sorong was not an "approved" target. We figured that, unbeknownst to any of us, Allied forces had been getting some valuable intelligence covertly from a secret "mole" in that location, well behind Japanese lines. Otherwise, why make a thing of it? Someone in Wing Headquarters was demanding to know the identity of the crew that had dropped the bombs.

Captain Jack Bratton of Union City, Tennessee, who had become squadron commander around the time we arrived at Fenton, was not about to get one of his crews in trouble over something this obscure. He asked Oman to work him up a reply through channels, but not to identify any 530th crew. Oman's first tongue-in-cheek draft delighted the air crewmen who saw it. It went like this: "Please pardon our Sorong. Nobody 'fesses up. See if they got a license number."

The leading sentence was a takeoff on the title of a popular movie, *Pardon My Sarong*. The mischievous message was rewritten, lest it offend Wing Headquarters officialdom. But, taking due notice, we were careful thereafter to preserve that village from bombing until further notice.

◉ ◉ ◉

ANDREW JACKSON BRATTON (he went by "Jack") was a popular commander. Among other things, he'd been known as a high school football star in western Tennessee while fullback at Union City High School. He fretted now that the aircrews, free from duties between missions, were getting too little exercise and too much sack time with so little to do there in the "middle of nowhere," as he described the barren territory.

Some of the guys, he thought—with so little in the way of diversion—might be staying up too late and drinking too much at the officers' club we'd built with bamboo about forty yards from the mess hall. Everybody got a weekly ration of two tall bottles of Australian beer, which didn't seem too grandly debilitating. But a lot of bartering went on. The Aussie anti-aircraft unit that moved into the area after our second bout with enemy bombers had access to additional beer, as well as two varieties of Australian bourbon. The Aussies loved American cigarettes (which we could buy, free of taxes, at the PX for five cents a pack). There soon developed an informal sort of bilateral trade pact that did a thriving business. We got all the beer we wanted and the Aussies got plenty of American cigarettes.

No bluenose, Bratton just wanted to keep us all on our toes, and in good physical shape. He discussed his concerns with me one day—"I don't want 'em all going soft," he said—and asked if I'd help him get a program together to keep the guys in shape. He said he wanted to appoint me "Squadron Athletic Officer." I didn't know there was any such job description, but I told him I'd help.

We got together a volunteer work brigade to clear off a baseball diamond, put up a second volleyball court, and organized some teams. Most of the fellows responded well to this, and a league of four teams quickly developed. The Aussies even tried to teach us cricket, which some enjoyed.

But the daily morning calisthenics decreed by the squadron commander got less than rave reviews. The call to join in was more a summons than an invitation. Bratton ordered everyone to participate unless medically excused or preparing for a mission. It was my job to preside over that daily routine. I also was supposed to take the roll, and that was fairly easy since we lined up by aircrew. But I don't remember that I ever turned in an attendance report. Maybe they all *supposed* I was turning in reports.

I'd brought a little lightweight speed bag in my B-4 luggage. Now we got a ring and a sturdy backdrop, and attached it all firmly at average eye level to a huge tree. I had a pair of lightweight bag gloves. Someone in quartermaster scrounged up two pairs of big 16-ounce boxing gloves. Some, though far from most, of the fellows enjoyed sparring. Bratton said, "Jim, you're responsible. But I damn sure don't want anybody up there on a bombing mission trying to breathe through an oxygen mask with a broken nose!"

No noses were broken, happily. And that was fortunate. We all routinely went on oxygen at any altitude over 10,000 feet. Often we'd fly in and make our bomb runs at high altitude to give Japanese anti-aircraft a more difficult target, but going to and coming from our bombing destinations, we almost always stayed under 10,000 feet. For one thing, it could be very cold in the higher altitudes. We had big, bulky, fleece-lined jackets and boots to protect us at the upper levels. Everyone, of course, had a parachute.

Our own crew had been fortunate in sustaining hardly any combat injuries—and no fatalities. About the worst any of us had suffered personally in aerial combat was a broken jaw on a replacement waist gunner, the result of a direct hit by a machine-gun shell fired from a Japanese Zero. Fortunately for our gunner, his assailant was far enough away when firing that the force of the shell was partly spent. Still, it fractured his jaw. The gunner went to the dispensary in Manbulloo for a fix and was grounded until it healed. In five weeks, he was back flying again.

LESS LUCKY THAT DAY were crewmen of our companion plane, *The Red Ass*, flown by our tent neighbor, Wilbur Morris, and manned by several of our crew's best buddies. On a pass over the

Japanese base at Langgoer, three of that crew were struck and injured by direct bursts of machine-gun fire.

Radio operator Sergeant Tom Carter was hit after being dispatched from his post to relieve the tailgunner. A burst of fire dislodged the tail-gun assembly, and the heavy 50-caliber machine-gun mount fell on Carter, crushing his leg and pinning him painfully in the cramped rear section of the plane. Both waist gunners—sergeants Delmar "Curley" Sprowls and Stanley Maslanka—were downed by a spray of bullets through the open waist windows.

Bombardier Paul Stansbury went back through the "cat walk" to check on the gunners when they didn't answer queries on the intercom. He found them in severe pain. Curley Sprowls had taken a shell through the left side of his face, shattering bones and knocking out several teeth. Maslanka bled profusely from a big, open wound where a Japanese bullet had torn into his shoulder.

To make matters worse, the crew discovered that all the painkiller medication was missing from the B-24's first-aid kits. This forced the three stricken airmen to suffer without relief on the way back. Wanting to get his crew to treatment as soon as possible, Morris put *The Red Ass* down at Darwin's RAAF base where permanent party Aussie medics maintained a hospital.

Stan Maslanka's shoulder injury was deemed sufficiently serious that he was sent back stateside for treatment. Carter recovered in three weeks from his leg injury. Sprowls underwent surgery and insisted on reporting back for duty. The unpretentious valor of young fellows like these gave quiet inspiration to the rest of us. Curley Sprowls was a special case in point.

Almost bald in his midtwenties (hence the nickname), Staff Sergeant Sprowls was thrice wounded and twice operated on. A barrel-chested Pennsylvanian who'd played some football at Penn State, Curley kept bouncing back. He was multi-rated and could handle just about any job on the airplane. He could operate the radio, was an excellent gunner, and an accomplished mechanic. Curley flew, in fact, with at least three different crews, including our own. Whenever a temporary sickness or injury created a vacancy of any sort, Curley was quickly there to volunteer. Before finishing his overseas tour of duty, he'd be awarded the Silver Star and the Purple Heart.

Soon thereafter, Bratton asked me to organize a group to construct an outdoor theater for the squadron. It wasn't hard to get volunteers for that detail! Curley Sprowls, not surprisingly, was among the first to offer his services. Most of our crowd hadn't seen a movie in a long while. Our cadre cleared a site within walking distance of all the 530th tents, erected a screen, and raised a platform to accommodate four or five escalating rows of plank seating, and a stand for the projector. Thereafter, when a film arrived, as a new one did about once a week, it had an enthusiastic audience.

MEANWHILE, FOLLOWING THE MISSION on which three wounded crewmen were forced to endure unnecessary suffering on the long homeward journey due to unaccountably missing painkiller medicine, Colonel Miller launched a quiet inquiry that yielded a stunning discovery.

On each of our Liberators was a discreet cubbyhole for the storage of first-aid medications, including a reportedly very efficacious drug (perhaps a morphine-based substance). Since this had been missing in the medicine kit aboard *The Red Ass*, Miller insisted on finding out whether any other of his aircraft suffered the same void. He was determined to learn whether the blame lay with a civilian source, or the quartermaster corps, or elsewhere—internally, perhaps?

To his dismay, his secret inspector discovered that several other aircraft kits were also specifically lacking the potent pain medication, but otherwise intact. It became apparent that the kits had been tampered with. Most of our aircraft retained the complete selection of nostrums, including the painkiller.

Someone had been robbing the kits. By the nature of things, the thefts would have had to occur on the flight line, which was loosely guarded much of the time. Consulting the logs of ground crew assignments revealed that one particular ground crew mechanic had recently been assigned to perform work on each of the affected aircraft.

The colonel's secret board of inquiry had its man. He was interrogated and confessed. He wasn't selling the drugs, but was a closet addict.

This whole thing must have been kept pretty well under wraps. By the time I learned of it, the mechanic had been relieved of duty and turned over to military police. Beyond that, I never learned his fate.

Lest anyone imagine this kind of episode was common in the Air Corps, let me hasten to stipulate that all the aircraft ground crewmen I knew were as dedicated to their aircraft, and those of us who flew them, as a pediatrician is to his patients. We depended on their skill and devotion.

As the B-24s kept bringing most of us safely home (even with the holes and pockmarks in the fuselage from enemy gunfire), we developed an ever-increasing respect for our big old "flying boxcars," as we'd called them earlier when comparing their square profile with that of the sleeker, sexier-looking B-17s so prevalent in the European theater.

The Liberators, with their four engines, longer range, and sturdy Davis wing design, were ideal for our mission, considering the distances between our targets. The greatest potential threats to our return from any mission were a hit by anti-aircraft, or a direct burst of fighter gunfire that would knock out an engine or rupture a fuel line, starting a fire or dissipating the gas we needed for our trip home.

Our companion squadron, the 531st, was dogged by foul luck. It had lost five crews in combat by the end of August. The group as a whole had suffered seventy-nine casualties by then, roughly 22 percent of our original air crewmen lost.

Once, returning from the Celebes, *Gus's Bus* took a hit in the nose area, causing the red hydraulic fuel that lubricated our landing gear to spurt and spray all over the bombardier's compartment. Unceremoniously drenched with the bright red stuff, I began desperately trying to find the holes in the line so I could somehow plug the flow. It would be a mighty hairy landing without operative landing gear to lower and lock our wheels. We'd have had to belly in, crushing hell out of the propellers and risking a gas tank explosion on impact. I turned around, and there was good ol' Kelly with his wrench. It was he, not I, who knew exactly how to stanch the flow before we lost all the fluid for our hydraulic system. When we put down safely at Fenton strip on still-functioning gear, a cheer went up from all of us for Kelly Koumarelos!

RABAUL HARBOR, in the Solomons, was probably the most hazardous bomb run in the South Pacific. It had earned the name "Suicide Alley," which bombing crews had learned to call it. Not only was the harbor heavily defended by an aggressive horde of veteran Zero, Zeke, and Oscar pilots; Rabaul's anti-aircraft gunners had been exposed to poundings for so long that they'd developed a fearsome and enviable skill in calculating altitude and blowing holes in U.S. aircraft. If we came over at 12,000 or even higher, it only meant we'd be in the scopes of their ground guns a trifle longer.

Another dreaded run was over Wewak up the east coast of New Guinea. Three of our 380th planes had suffered hits from anti-aircraft bursts above Rabaul, and two while crossing the targets of Wewak. A sort of legend had evolved about a mythical gunner at Wewak. We ruefully called him "One-Shot Charley."

We were growing up, rapidly. War is a fast track to maturity. Confronted almost daily with the certainty of death, we might have been learning a bit also about the uncertainties of life. Almost all the air crewmen were in our twenties, some of us just barely. We'd have contested anyone who judged us too young. Every one of us had volunteered for combat service. It is hard to know whether we'd have been this patriotic had the Japanese not attacked Pearl Harbor, and with such cunning duplicity. We knew the odds, and accepted them.

# 15

## BALIKPAPAN!

ON AUGUST 13, 1943, we blew up the oil refineries at Balikpapan, Borneo. That became a turning point of sorts in the Pacific War. In daring it, we inflicted major damage on the enemy, and set a new world record in the process. It was the decisive, defining moment of change in the Pacific War's momentum.

Our plan was bold. No bombing crew, anywhere, had ever flown that far and back—2,700 miles—to hit a target. The round trip from our base in northern Australia would consume seventeen hours. Each of our eleven B-24s would carry 3,500 gallons of fuel, just enough to get there and back, leaving room in each plane for only six 500-pound bombs.

At the briefing, our Group Commander Col. William A. Miller, said, "We're going to do something that has never been done. We're going to fly the longest bombing mission on record, and when we're through, the Japs will be the ones running out of gas!" The Balikpapan facility, we were told, supplied most of Japan's aviation fuel and lubricating oil.

For two months, we had harassed our enemy's military installations all across the crescent that surrounds Australia's northern tip. Those blows had been like a boxer's left jabs, to confuse, tire, and discombobulate an opponent. It was time now to go to the body with heavy poundings, to take the spring from his legs and rob his lungs of endurance. "Kill the body and the head will go" was a long-established axiom of the ring.

Col. Miller prepared us well. As we huddled there in the group briefing room, his eyes sparkled with controlled excitement.

"It's time to start cutting the legs out from under the Japs," Miller said, "and you are the ones who can do it." After the briefest pause, he grinned. "Correction! *We* are the ones who can do it."

"Right on, Colonel!" someone shouted, and a cheer went up. An upbeat mood swept across the room as Miller smiled broadly. He'd just made clear that he and his crew would be flying with us. We sensed that he was proud and excited over the challenge. As he explained the mission, orienting us with the target and chosen air route by the large roll-down maps, his enthusiasm became contagious.

"So everybody had better be well slept," Miller concluded. "No partying—repeat, *no partying* tomorrow night. And I mean that. Bunk time and lights out for everybody no later than twenty-one hundred hours tomorrow night." In Air Corps jargon, that meant 9 P.M.

On mission day we took off midmorning, and flew first to Darwin. There we refueled, topping off the wing tanks and installing two auxiliary tanks in the bomb rack areas of each aircraft. The Australians fed us a good lunch, and Aussie ground crews serviced our B-24s.

Fuel was the *sine qua non*—our mission's purpose and its indispensable element. As we gathered speed for takeoff on the Darwin runway, about five o'clock that afternoon, we were hoping to begin arriving over Balikpapan shortly after midnight. We felt confident we had enough gas to get us to target and back but knew there was none to spare. Takeoffs were timed five minutes apart. Our crew was either first or second in the air.

At twenty minutes after midnight, *Gus's Bus* was first to reach the target area. A hole in the loose flotilla of overhead clouds gave us a perfect sight of the refinery complex with its rows of big oil and gasoline storage tanks. To my amazement, ground lights were illuminating the tanks and buildings. The crosshairs of my bombsight locked onto the dead center of the tank installations during a surprisingly steady bomb run. There was no flak, not yet, no interceptors in the air. They hadn't expected us.

We banked to the right, following "bombs away," circling back on the seaward side of Balikpapan to begin our homeward course. Below, two separate storage tanks were ablaze. Black smoke billowed. All the ground lights now were out, but our tank fires lighted the area. We'd hit our mark.

Then came the anti-aircraft fire and a swarm of Zeros. As individual bomb runs continued for an hour or more, our later-arriving crews would have to fight off succeeding waves of Japanese fighters. But we left the refinery a flaming inferno, and several large Japanese supply ships lay at the bottom of the harbor.

Our most nervous time came as daylight set in. Crossing the shoreline west of Darwin, we crossed our fingers, uncertain if there was enough fuel to get us home.

WHEN WE TOOK COUNT in the morning hours after landing, all except one of the eleven Liberators had made it home safely. By morning the news at the operations shack was that *Shady Lady*, piloted by Douglas Craig, reportedly had been attacked by a persistent formation of Zeros near Timor, and consumed precious fuel evading the attackers. According to radio signals, the plane barely made it to Australia, where Craig had to set the sputtering ship down on a sand dune in the unoccupied outback.

At midday, three crews (including ours) took off to reconnoiter the general area indicated by the radio signals and ferret out, if we could, the route the downed plane would have followed. Finally, after about an hour's flying and looking, we spotted it. The grounded crew, having heard our engines, surrounded their inert aircraft, waving wildly to attract our attention. Passing over at low altitude, we saw the conspicuous sign they'd made on the open turf, using silk from their parachutes. Three huge white letters, on the reddish soil—$H_2O$—advertised their most pressing need. They were out of water. Thirst reigned under the bright Australian sun. To them, the air must have seemed hot enough to dry spit before it reached the ground.

We'd anticipated this, as well as probable hunger. More than twenty-four hours had elapsed since their last meal, by our calculations. We were carrying two good-sized sturdy water containers and some baskets of sandwiches. We made a low bombing pass, releasing the water and food. The containers skidded in, about fifty yards from the downed plane.

Then we returned toward a road where we'd seen Aussie rescue trucks scouting for the plane or survivors. Signaling them to follow, we led the rescuers to the plane. This happy reward was the icing on the cake! The sort of stuff that made choking down the drier crumbs of life worthwhile. Some kind fate had decreed that we'd find these colleagues, so like ourselves, lost out there, dehydrating from thirst and probably growing frantic in the barren wasteland.

What a splendid satisfaction! Now all eleven crews—110 men—were accounted for. More even than the memory of the gaudy conflagration at Balikpapan, it is this that keeps the moment vital in my mind these more than sixty years later. On the way back to Fenton, sleepy as we were, our faces wouldn't quit grinning.

*The author as an Aviation Cadet, Santa Ana, California AAB, July, 1942.*

*Crew portrait, El Paso, February 1943. Author, front row, 2nd from left.*

*Visitor from Australian High Command conferring in Fenton, Summer 1943.*

Lt. Col. Bill Miller, arm in sling from runway accident, and other survivors.
Fenton, 380th Hg. Bldg., Fall 1943.

Alley Oop, *the aircraft
flown by Lt. Joe Vick that
cracked up in a landing
accident, killing four
passengers and injuring
Col. Miller.*

*Nose art on* Gypsy, *lead
plane flown by Group
Commander William S.
Miller in 170-plane raid on
Cape Gloucester, December
26, 1943.*

1st Lt. Pat Mullins, navigator for Gus's Bus, 1943.

Capt. Augustus V. Connery and "the bus," after multiple bombing missions, noted in nose art, December 1943, Dobodura, New Guinea.

The crew, Fenton Airfield, Australia, fall 1943. Author kneeling, front row, left. Note Connery with "Smokey," the crew mascot.

Lt. Hal Grace, bombardier on
Fyrtle Myrtle, *shot down over
Makasar, captured by Japanese
and beheaded September 1943.*

*1st* Lt. David Lippencott, pilot.
*He and his crew were shot
down, captured, and beheaded
by Japanese, September 1943.*

*Yanks and Aussies at Fenton toasting with bottles of Aussie beer.*

*Wreckage of* Little Joe *at edge of coral reef, photographed from the air one year later.*

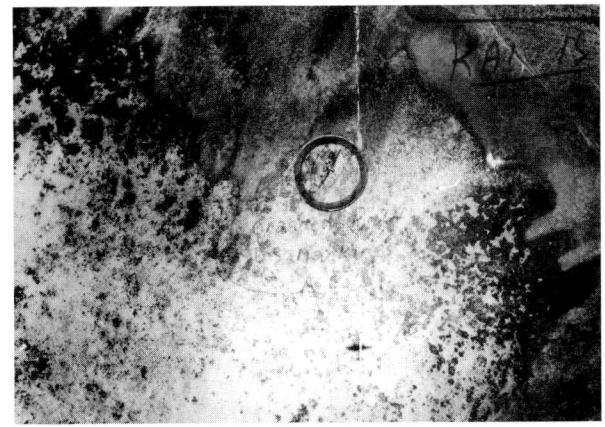

*Lt. Edward Skuzinski, navigator, injured and disabled in crash of* Little Joe, *left by Japanese to perish inside plane at end of coral reef in rising tide—on his birthday—September 11, 1943.*

*Lt. Paul Stansbury, bombardier on* Little Joe. *Shot down September 21, 1943, P.O.W.*

*Co-pilot, 1st Lt. Bob Russell, original member of crew. Shot down while flying with Wilbur Morris crew September 21, 1943. Captured, P.O.W.*

*The author, right, on return from overseas, visits with old friend and college classmate Lt. Joe Sutton.*

*Lt. Ervin Mellinger, bombardier on* Prince Valiant *on August 17, 1943. Wounded over Balikpapan Harbor by 20mm cannon shot, he maintained concentration and completed his bomb run, hitting and sinking a Japanese tanker, then extinguished flames in B-24 nose compartment single-handedly.*

*Gus*

Gus's Bus *on bombing mission, Celebes Islands, Summer 1943.*

*1st Lt. Harold S. Mulhollen, pilot. Killed in action January 1944.*

*Actor Gary Cooper and troupe arriving at Fenton airstrip to entertain troops, Christmas 1943.*

*Aborigines in hunting mode, Northern Australia, 1943.*

*Half-grown wallaby, a crewman's pet, at Fenton Strip, Fall 1943.*

# 16

## *SHADY LADY* AND ANGELS OF THE DESERT

THERE WAS A LOT MORE about the *Shady Lady* adventure that we didn't know, and never could have dreamed. Two days later, reuniting with some of that crew, we got the whole story. It was a bigger drama than we'd imagined, one in which we'd played merely a bit part. We were not the first rescuers to sight the downed aircraft. We learned of a harrowing series of bizarre events that dogged the plane's trail that night—and we discovered to our delight that there are angels of mercy in the Australian outback.

The fellows who made up *Shady Lady*'s crew had drawn the unenviable "ass-end Charlie" assignment. Drafted to come in dead last over Balikpapan, they'd also been expected to take aerial photographs of the target area, appraising what damage the raid had wrought.

Weather did not cooperate with our ill-starred cleanup hitters. Heavy storms inland from the harbor had accelerated during the raid, high winds and overhead clouds moving swiftly from landward and over the refinery complex. The winds picked up billowing waves of thick, black smoke that belched from the fires our bombs had set in the ruptured oil tanks, sending these smoke shields up and out over the harbor and directly into *Shady Lady*'s line of flight.

When the crew arrived at Borneo's coastal line, its members had no visibility at all of the target area or any ground-level installations. Navigator John Nash had to alter the original flight plan. In order to escape the great blinding drafts of acrid smoke, Nash had to plot a wide circular detour around the oncoming tide of blackness, pass high across the harbor, well beyond the target area, and then come back with the tailwind from the interior land mass. But this maneuver, of course, consumed more time and burned more fuel.

Finally, flying downwind and able to see the area below, bombardier Randall Packard began a bomb run on the now-blazing tank farm, and RAAF Flight Officer Sandy Rustin, attached to the unit for photographic purposes, began to train his camera on the most promising scenes in the bedlam below.

Suddenly a huge ground-based searchlight settled its piercing glare on *Shady Lady*, half blinding both pilot and bombardier, and attracting bursts of fire from Japanese anti-aircraft batteries. After barely escaping two flash explosions so close the airplane wobbled from detonation waves, pilot Doug Craig manually overrode the Norden bombsight flight controls, aborting the ill-fated run in favor of swift, forceful evasive action. Craig threw the big bird into a series of strenuous dives and turns.

As a result, the plane fortuitously eluded destruction while explosive noises and shocks sounded all about, until *Shady Lady* outran the roving searchlight and the guns were stilled. The violent darts and turns of the aircraft, however, had thrown bombardier Packard harshly into the hard Plexiglas and metal surfaces of the nose cone, where he'd been bending intently over the bombsight. Not only was Packard badly bruised by the sudden upending, but the aircraft's intercom system had somehow ceased to function, presumably disrupted by either a stray enemy projectile or an electrical malfunction.

Although now seriously handicapped by their inability to converse with one another during a second bomb run, both pilot Craig and bombardier Packard were determined to try again. On their next pass, they once more caught the spotlight, but continued dead ahead through a steady bomb run, and two of Packard's bombs landed squarely, igniting more storage tanks.

It was two o'clock in the morning when the dogged crew cleared the target area and began the long trek home. They still weren't out of trouble. They'd spent a total of forty-five precious minutes over and around Balikpapan and were wondering nervously now if their fuel supply would hold out.

Their initial plan had been to pursue an evasive course en route home so as to avoid being spotted in the early morning hours by enemy interceptors stationed at Koepang. They briefly attempted a more westerly detour, in fact, but were turned back by the pyrotechnics of a fierce electrical storm. In the process, more time and fuel were wasted.

Now, in view of their time-aggravated fuel problem, Craig and Nash both knew it would be impossible to make it home unless they followed the shortest, straightest, most direct route. And this, they realized, would lead them directly over southwestern Timor and the Koepang airdrome.

As the solitary B-24 approached the forbidden area, a flight of three Japanese Zeke interceptors took off to check out the intruder. To the relief of the whole crew, the Zeke pilots flew beneath the B-24's flight altitude, carefully out of range of its guns, until it was apparent that the Liberator was not on a bomb run. Finally, *Shady Lady* intersected a big cloud bank and headed directly into and through it, poor practice generally but essential at this point. When the plane finally emerged back into the open, the Zekes had disappeared. The crew was vastly relieved. They had a secret they desperately didn't want the Zeke pilots to fathom.

Apparently, the Japanese pilots had respected the firepower of the four-engine bomber, assuming its gunners were fully armed and ready to repel them.

The big fear still remained. Doug Craig had "leaned down" the engines as far as he safely could to conserve the remaining slim supply of fuel. The crew had been aloft for eighteen hours, the last nine intermittently sparked with high tension. As they approached the Australian coastline, an engine sputtered. The pilot knew they'd never make it to home base.

Craig picked the nearest flatland clearing he could see in the morning haze and put *Shady Lady* down in what looked like dry sandy land on the opposite side of a billabong. It was, at last and at least, Australia. Doug couldn't have known he was landing in a salt flat. The soft salt-sand mix grabbed and held the landing-gear tires even as the engines' remaining forward power pulled the body of the vehicle away from the bog. Under the stress, the nose gear collapsed and the plane tossed forward, breaking propellers and lurching to an awkward nose-down stop.

They'd landed. The plane was not operational for takeoff. But they'd made it! The crew was safe, though tossed about, sore, and dog-tired. Exhausted!

No sight or sound of human habitation in the immediate environs, Craig assigned two crewmen to sentry duty so that others could sleep or rest while the radioman tapped out their location and surfed for rescuers. *Dit.Dit.Dit.—Daaa.Daaa.Daaa.—Dit.Dit.Dit.* He kept trying Fenton's call numbers.

Waist gunner Maurice Powers, while serving as sentry, couldn't keep his mind from revisiting the stunning events of that unforgettable night. "Slim" Powers, as he was affectionately called by crewmates and other airmen, was a popular character at the 529th, known for his jovial nature and entertaining sense of the ridiculous. At one point during the nerve-chilling moments when *Shady Lady* was spotlighted by the enemy searchlight, Powers had loosened up the crew with his own brand of comic relief. Slim had assumed the role of an actor acknowledging applause. Standing in the spotlighted open window, he had bowed ceremoniously to an imagined adoring crowd below, intoning the words "Thank you! Thank you very much!" The waist-gun crowd broke up in laughter, momentarily forgetting fright. Fun to remember. But—what was that?

Quickly, now, Slim's mind snapped back to the present. Was it human movement that slipped past the corner of his eye, or the shadow of a cloud? He turned his head to look.

Looming there, at a distance of maybe thirty yards, stood three figures, motionless as statues, observing the fallen plane. To Slim, their appearance was menacing.

The three were Aborigines. Clad sparingly for hunting—almost naked, in fact—they carried boomerangs and what looked like long spears. The sergeant, who'd learned just a few words of native dialect, attempted an Aboriginal salutation, nervously trying to sound friendly.

"Good morning," came the courteous response, in perfect English. A wave of relief washed over Powers. Meeting others of the crew and seeing their plight, the party's leader dispatched one of the other two to go for help. The wiry youth left in a dead run, disappearing over the horizon. He returned in an hour or so, accompanied by a tall Caucasian who looked to be in his late twenties.

The new arrival, as it turned out, was a Benedictine monk named Seraphim Sanz. A native of Spain, Father Sanz had come to the Australian outback a few years earlier. Along with six others of his order and three nuns, he served a small mission at a remote site called Kalumburu. From there, the little cadre maintained a lonely vigil in that vast, parched stretch of coastal land sparsely inhabited by Aborigines, occasional kangaroo herds, wild dingoes, and large ants that built tall earthen mounds.

Sanz saw to it that the crew was cared for, fed and watered, their wounds and ailments looked at, and that contact was made with Australian army rescue units. I never learned, in fact, whether the trucks we'd aerially helped guide to the crippled plane's location had been alerted by our Air Corps people at Fenton or by Father Sanz's radio hookup at Kalumburu.

It didn't matter. Our pals were safe.

But the knowledge of the monks' lonely work at that remote outpost in the outback intrigued me. I would learn that at least six separate rescues of Aussie and American troops were credited to that one unassuming man, Father Seraphim Sanz.

He had made friends with the native population. Kalumburu mission personnel treated their wounds, taught them English, sometimes shared rations with them. Whenever they came upon stranded personnel, the natives knew exactly where to go for help.

A year earlier, Father Sanz and his clerical colleagues had helped rescue 120 Australian seamen after Japanese bombed and sank their ship off the northwestern Australian coast. Mission personnel organized, oversaw, and worked alongside an Aborigine work crew to build by hand an auxiliary airstrip at Kalumburu. It served our forces as a refueling and bomb-loading base.

These activities resulted in fierce Japanese retaliation. Several times, planes from Koepang and Japanese carriers strafed and bombed the Benedictine mission. Following one such assault that would come three months later, in September 1943, Australian security forces noted that Father Sanz was absent when the air strike came, and drew suspicious assumptions.

The fierce Japanese bombing attack killed six, including the monk superior, while seriously damaging the mission building. In the momentary hysteria, some military security people accused Father Sanz, the only absent member at the time of the Japanese raid, of knowing the attack was coming. Hints arose that he was an enemy spy. It was known that he, a Spanish native, could send and receive coded messages by Air Force radio.

The truth was that Sanz's absence from the mission at the time of the Japanese attack was easily explained. He had been sent to Groome, 600 miles distant, for badly needed supplies, making the twelve-day journey in the mission's old sailing lugger with a broken mast. Adding injury to insult, Sanz and his Aboriginal helper had to load the several tons of goods by hand and pump all night to keep the leaky old lugger afloat.

Security authorities, learning the truth, apologized publicly to the priest for the unwarranted accusation. Years later, Sanz would be officially cited by the Australian government for extraordinary patriotic service to the nation. The last I heard, in 2002, Father Sanz, then eighty-eight, was the only surviving member of the wartime contingent at Kalumburu mission.

In 1988, celebrating the sesquicentennial of Australia's nationhood, a number of us from the old 380th made it back to Australia. There were lots of sentimental remembrances. Two members of the *Shady Lady* crew were flown back to the site of the rescue, where the big plane came down in the sandy, salty soil. There they met again with Father Sanz and reminisced. But I'm getting ahead of my story.

Something about this whole episode intrigued me unforgettably. For all our masculine bluster and protestations of self-reliance, it is strangely comforting to have some fleeting evidence, here and there, of guardian angels in unexpected places.

Oh, yes, and thanks in part to Sanz and that group of romance rangers at the mission, and to the extraordinary skills and toil of too often unsung ground maintenance people, *Shady Lady* was fully repaired, flown back to base, and put back on active duty. With that, the Balikpapan raid chalks up a ten-strike. All 110 crewmen safe and all eleven planes in inventory.

A fitting footnote to this story lingers yet. On July 29, 2000, a reporter for the *West Australian* wrote, " . . . the tyre marks of the Liberator could still be seen in the salt pan." Forty-five years later!

I think I believe it.

# 17

## THROWING THE LONG BALL

THE BALIKPAPAN MISSION was a major milepost in the Pacific War, and a foretaste of things to come. It was like playing on a team whose coach discovered the successful forward pass toward the end of the second quarter and couldn't wait to throw more long ones. After that raid on Balikpapan, all of us in the 380th enjoyed a shared anticipation of putting big new numbers on the scoreboard. That mission would bring the group our first Presidential Unit Citation. Its results would inspire more long, strategic raids.

Col. Miller, encouraged by uniformly positive reports from the returning crews, was anxious to discover, in daylight, just how much actual damage we had inflicted that night. So, I suppose, were higher-ups in the command chain. To get a clearer picture, Miller sent two crews on a special photographic and reconnaissance mission. The crews of Captain Jack Banks, 528th, and Lieutenant Howard Hahn of the 531st took off from Darwin at two o'clock on the morning of August 16. Less than three days had passed since the return of the eleven bombing crews.

Supplied with photographic equipment and accompanied by trained photographers and intelligence specialists, the two Liberators each carried 3,700 gallons of gasoline, 7,000 rounds of ammunition, and only three 100-pound bombs. Expecting to need slightly more loiter time over target than our eleven bombing crews had expended, they carried even more fuel and less bomb weight. Anxious not to be detected en route by enemy forces at Timor or Makassar, they charted a route that gave those sites a wide berth and flew those segments at an unusually low altitude to avoid being seen.

Good weather provided perfect conditions for aerial photography. As they began their first photo run over the target at ten o'clock that morning, the big oil drums below were still burning from the fires ignited by our bombs two nights earlier. Presence of the first arriving B-24, once noted, evoked anti-aircraft fire. It was Banks's 528th plane, *Miss Giving*. In spite of the cannonading, it completed the photo run unscathed. Sighting a 3,000-ton freighter at dock in the harbor, bombardier Clint McWilliams asked permission for a bomb run. His three relatively small bombs made a good enough hit to tear a hole in the big boat's side, and it settled to the bottom of the harbor.

*Miss Giving* was attacked by eight Japanese Zero fighters that gave chase as the bomber flew out to sea. The attackers scored one cannon shot that knocked out the number-three engine in a running battle that lasted almost an hour. The gunners aboard the B-24 destroyed three Zeros. All went careening crazily, aflame, into the sea. Limping back on three engines, the crew of the crippled craft spotted more fighters rising to attack in the vicinity of Timor, but shook the interceptors by taking cover in a fortuitous cloud bank. Their fuel supply was by now precariously low. The crew donned parachute gear as the plane crossed land, but the landing at Fenton was safe—except that the number-one engine sputtered out while taxiing to the revetment.

The other plane, flown by Hahn, had come over Balikpapan a few minutes after the initial photo run. Defenders, by then, were ready. *She 'Asta*, the 531st ship, was attacked almost immediately. Its crew downed one Zero, dropped its bombs on an ammo dump, and returned safely with the desired photos.

Photographic evidence of destruction at the refinery was impressive. The pictures confirmed that our first raid had seriously disrupted Japan's oil and aviation gas supply for the region. But the evidence of a large flotilla of juicy new shipping targets was too inviting to forego a second full-scale raid on Balikpapan. Photos of the harbor revealed fifteen or twenty commercial freighters and transports in the bay, consisting of at least 70,000 tons of shipping capacity. This was too attractive a strategic target to let slip through our fingers.

THE NEW NAME OF THE GAME was to cripple Japan's ability to supply its forward troops. If we could dry up our enemy's fuel and shipping capacities in the Southwest Pacific, that surely would hasten the day when General MacArthur's ground forces could begin to retake land. The Japanese army of occupation would grow daily more vulnerable if we could pinch off vital supply lines now stretched out across the islands of the Pacific.

And so, a second full-fledged assault on Balikpapan was ordered. There was no time to waste if we wanted to deliver a crippling blow before those ships could guess our plan and disperse. The new raid would launch the following night, August 17. It would be carried out by eleven crews that hadn't participated in the first attack. As before, the planes would strike at night. Only this time, the primary target would be the shipping armada in the harbor.

The eleven crews ran into bad weather. Two planes, consuming excessive fuel while their pilots and navigators sought a less threatening route, were forced to abort the mission and return. One crew, not to waste the opportunity, dropped its bombs on the Makassar airdrome.

This time, Balikpapan's defenses were primed and ready. Each of the nine remaining crews encountered heavy flak and active interception by formations of Zekes and Zeros. But hunting was good in the harbor. Several of our Liberators came in at low level. A 529th crew, led by Captain Bob Horn, was first to score a direct hit on a freighter. A second, flown by Lieutenant Jim Soderberg, suffered a hit by anti-aircraft cross fire while bombardier Jack Garlock was completing a bomb run that sank a second freighter. Two of that crew gave all their attention to putting out fires in the bomb bay with fire extinguishers. In the end, they were successful and limped home safely.

In a third, a former classmate of mine named Ervin Mellinger, bombardier on the B-24 dubbed *Prince Valiant,* took shot from a 20-millimeter cannon shell that burst through the nose compartment during the final seconds of his bomb run. Wounded, Erv never lost concentration on his bombsight. His lethal load hit and destroyed the tanker that was its target. Fire broke out in the plane's nose section. Though in pain, Erv managed to extinguish the flames.

*Prince Valiant's* problems were not over. The number-one engine, struck by flak, was losing oil pressure. Pilot Bob Fleming feathered the propeller and headed home on the remaining three engines. On route, the number-two engine went out. This presented a serious problem. Even those who haven't had to do it must know that it is extremely difficult to maintain altitude, speed, and guidance in a four-engined aircraft when the only two operative engines are on the same side of the plane.

With neither power plant working on the left side, pilot Bob Fleming and his whole crew exhibited superb airmanship in nursing the crippled bomber to Darwin, where they landed it. In recognition of their feat, the British government did an extraordinary thing: It awarded Fleming a Distinguished Flying Cross of the United Kingdom.

Wounded crewmen returned in about half the B-24s that participated that night, but none of ours were killed. Once again, 110 aloft and 110 back alive. Phenomenally great luck! Our fellows in the 380th had inflicted additional damage to the oil refinery and sunk 30,000 tons of shipping that night, without losing a man.

WE'D BEEN INFINITELY LUCKIER in this regard than our 8th Air Force counterparts in North Africa. Just a couple of weeks before our first Balikpapan raid, a fleet of 178 B-24s took off from Libya on a thirteen-hour round-trip mission covering 2,400 miles (almost as long as ours) to bomb the oil refineries at Ploesti, Romania.

Their goal was the same as ours: knock out the enemy's main oil and fuel source. Churchill had called Ploesti "the taproot of German might." It supplied about a third of Hitler's needs. Considering the number of aircraft and crews committed to that effort, the stakes were even higher.

Their method of attack, and the ghastly losses they suffered, differed widely from our experience. It was their plan to come in only 300 feet off the ground, escaping early detection for a massive low-level attack. It was a daring idea, and they hit a lot of big oil drums.

The only trouble was that their strikes set off both primary and secondary explosions. The detonation waves erupted just as second and later lines of our huge bomber fleet were crossing directly overhead. The tragic toll on U.S. bombers was devastating!

In all, the Ploesti raid did great damage to Hitler's oil supply but exacted a terrible cost—ninety bombers failed to return that night, some wrecked with their crews taken prisoner. On August 1, 1943—later known as "Black Sunday"—446 American crewmen were killed or missing in action, and 130 wounded.

Reviewing these grim statistics, we thanked our lucky stars that the lives of all our 220 crewmen on the two Balikpapan raids had been spared. The economics of scale were quite different between Japan and Germany, but we had been blessed with good fortune.

We'd have to return to Balikpapan from time to time to keep the industrious Japanese from restoring the facility, but we were off to a good start. And there were, within our extended flight range, other industrial targets to destroy before the enemy would be brought down.

ENCOURAGED BY THESE SUCCESSES, the 380th embarked on a series of long strategic raids. Three in which our crew participated slammed the region's other oil refinery near Surabaya, Java, and its nearby naval base (almost as far west of our home strip as Borneo was to the northwest), a complex of busy facilities on Makassar, and the nickel plant at Pomelaa, in the Celebes east of Borneo. All of these were long flights, and in each we managed to deal another body blow to the industrial and shipping base that supported the forward flank of Japan's war machine.

Surabaya was home to an important naval station with a huge port in the Flores Sea. Across that sea and due south from the mouth of the Makassar Strait, it was one of Japan's busiest shipping centers. It lay in a wide, sweeping natural harbor. The large oil refinery at nearby Tiepoe was second only to Balikpapan's in production capacity. These facilities were defended by an active air base. Three targets altogether—refinery, harbor, and airdrome—made the northern Java coast an inviting destination for several group missions.

To give our B-24s legs long enough to reach that faraway site, we had to fly several hundred miles across the red Iron Range to western Australia's coastline. There, near a little town named Marble Bar, which reminded me of movies about the old American West, we'd land and refuel. Our Aussie hosts had built a supposedly secret airstrip. It was called Corunna Downs, and it was a fairly primitive installation to be serving as the launching pad for aircraft as big as the Liberators. Barely long enough for our takeoffs and landings, the paved strip ended in a slight rise that made it hard for the pilots to see what lay over the rim until we were airborne.

But we made the best of this, and our crew had the good fortune to survive both anti-aircraft fire and attacks by Oscars, Zekes, and Zeros, the three most prevalent types of Japanese fighters in the Surabaya region. We grew fairly good at recognizing enemy airplanes by type—but not good enough. Once, returning from a daylight mission to Makassar, we encountered a big surprise when all of us on *Gus's Bus* misidentified a flight of approaching aircraft. That mistake almost cost us our lives.

# 18

## QUESTIONS OF IDENTITY, HUMOR, AND HONOR

"LOOK!" SOMEONE SHOUTED over the intercom. "P-thirty-eights. About ten o'clock. P-thirty-eights!" We all exclaimed in amazement. There, off ahead and slightly to the left came a formation of three familiar twin-fuselaged silhouettes, the shape that so distinctively characterized our sleek two-engined American fighter model, the P-38. How did they get way out here, we wondered? We were easily twice the distance of a P-38's range from Darwin.

We were idly speculating as to where these three could be based (one of the guys wondered aloud if we had an aircraft carrier in the region) when the formation made a frontal pass at us, spitting machine-gun and cannon fire. Certain that the planes were "friendlies," we hadn't gotten off a single shot at them.

Now wary, we watched these aircraft circle widely to our right, gaining altitude until they'd blurred into an invisible spot somewhere directly between our location and the sun. Though we couldn't see them at all now for the sun's brilliant glare, we knew they'd be coming again. They'd be hurtling at us right out of the sky's bright ball of fire. Two voices shouted at once as the hostile fighters closed on us fast from about three o'clock high, and all of our right-side guns fired.

We should have hit at least one of the three, but we saw nothing to let us confirm that we had. They disappeared as quickly as they'd come at us, somewhere low at about seven o'clock. For the next thirty minutes we all stayed on edgy alert, expecting another attack from the sun's westerly direction, or maybe a sudden spurt of speed from behind one of the little cumulus clouds that floated off to our left like a small flock of sheep.

But nothing further happened. The interceptors, after two passes, may have begun running low on fuel and returned to base. Or, we just might have downed or crippled one. We'll never know. What we did know was that our American P-38 wasn't the only aircraft so configured. Every guy on our crew had undergone extensive drilling in aircraft recognition. We'd been tested, over and over again, observing rapidly flashing silhouettes until we supposed we were proficient in swiftly, and correctly, identifying both friendly and enemy fighter aircraft.

BACK AT BASE, we spilled our story out to Group Intelligence. Nobody else had seen any such plane, and there were no American P-38s stationed anywhere remotely near us. Finally, someone in G-2 came up with a silhouette and new data sheet on an Italian-made fighter with twin fuselages. Its profile was almost indistinguishable from our P-38, only smaller in size. Whether some of those had been given to the Japanese, or a squadron of Italian aviators had been deployed to the Pacific (which seemed doubtful), we never found out. At least I never did.

Our crew took some good-humored ribbing over the incident. Some of our compatriots insisted on knowing what we'd been carrying in our water canteens aboard ship. Others suggested we might have spotted a formation of giant dragonflies, or maybe spaceships left over from Orson Welles's radio extravaganza of 1938. Mock verbal disparagement of this sort, exchanged between crews, was a fairly constant staple around our tent city in the outback. It helped preserve our sanity by making it impossible for anybody to take himself too seriously.

ANOTHER TIME WE TOOK a spate of gentle needling involving a Japanese aircraft we'd shot down. One day as we approached Kendari, our target on the eastern side of the Celebes peninsula that juts out into the Banda Sea, a Japanese military aircraft was rising from the airstrip, gaining altitude directly in our path of flight. It was not an interceptor and did not look like a bomber, certainly not a large one. It had two engines and resembled one of our C-47s in size and shape.

We knew only that it was a military airplane because of the mottled camouflage color and the telltale red ball, representing the rising sun, that marked all Japanese military planes. Since it was crossing right in front of us, we had the drop on it. Several of us got off a few rounds. John Tackett, flying in the circularly mobile top turret, continued to fire as the Japanese plane crossed toward the left. It burst into flames from a direct hit and headed, nose first, into the sea. Connery took a snapshot of the odd-looking plane as it dove, trailing a tail of vapor reminiscent of a comet.

From this, and our verbal descriptions, debriefers identified the plane as a Kawasaki K-45, usually used as a military transport vehicle. Other crews recognized good heckling material. Quickly they began to shame us for gunning down an "unarmed" plane. One or two of the bolder hecklers began to question how we should portray it in our plane's nose art—bomb figures for ground targets destroyed, airplane silhouettes for downed Japanese fighters. Since it wasn't an interceptor aircraft, and it wasn't a ship we'd sunk, our self-appointed convention of critics voted that we should paint on our forward fuselage, along with the few legitimate trophies we'd accumulated, the image of a duck.

By a queer quirk of circumstance, someone in A-2 (Air Wing Intelligence) sent word of an intercepted Japanese report that certain officials of Nippon's South Pacific command had been conferring over strategy in Kendari. On departure, according to the message, the Kawasaki K-45 in which they traveled had been lost to enemy gunfire. At least, that was the shape of the story when I heard it. By the time it circulated through camp, gathering momentum as stories will, the hapless planeload that ran afoul of *Gus's Bus* included General Tojo's second in command and Emperor Hirohito's first cousin. Needless to say, nobody on Connery's crew took any action to slow the progression of the self-inflating rumor.

ONCE, AS WE JOINED a large contingent attacking Surabaya via the desolate strip at Corunna Downs, we learned that we were to include among our passengers the former Dutch governor of Java and Sumatra. The governor and his entire ruling coterie had been driven out, forced to flee Java just ahead of the advancing Japanese.

Now, with twenty or so Flying Circus aircraft prepared to rain tons of destruction on the harbor, the refinery, and the airdrome, the former governor from the Netherlands was asking to go with us. Moreover, he wanted to drop thousands of printed circulars reminding the native Indonesian population that he'd said he would return, and the equivalent of "Well, here I am!"

The circulars would implore local citizens to have hope, resist the evil Japanese, and commit whatever sabotage might enter their minds, awaiting the triumphal return of their friends from Holland. At least, this is what I *think* the circulars said. I could not translate them, and didn't try. It was decided, by what logic I knew not, that the distinguished guest should ride in *Gus's Bus*. Further, someone reasoned that since *Gus's Bus* would be flying low to drop the leaflets, we should carry no bombs as that might compromise the governor's message.

The weather was miserable over Java that night, with high winds, pyrotechnics, and lashing rain. Our higher-flying bomber aircraft had trouble spotting their targets because of the inclement conditions, and our crew had to fly in low enough to identify population centers over which to release the governor's public-relations initiative. You have, no doubt, already imagined the ribbing we took from brother crews upon our return. The kinder ones suggested we should have worn frock coats and striped pants, since we'd quit being warriors and become diplomats.

THE RAINS CAME in the fall. Northern Australia had been almost bone-dry for the past eight months. The paucity—virtual absence, in fact—of rainfall reminded me of far West Texas. While the drought held, it seemed even more arid. Then, suddenly, two monsoons came one after the other. The first monsoon season was blissfully short, with a slow, miserable drizzle falling constantly, night and day, for what I remember as about three weeks. The second monsoon had an entirely different character. It didn't rain throughout most of the day, but at approximately five o'clock every afternoon a dark speck would appear on the horizon, which meant that we'd better take cover. Within five minutes the sky would be filled with hard, wind-driven rainfall that might last for thirty minutes and then be gone.

The wet season, for all its depressing character, provided us with a few mirthful moments. In the early summer we'd dug slit trenches, at least four feet deep, for our protection during Japanese air raids. These trenches now, with no invitation from us, were filled with water. Almost every night, as most of us lay in our bunks with the tent flaps always rolled up so we could catch any vagrant breeze, we'd hear at least one loud outcry of wounded dignity. We knew that another brave soul on his way back in the dark, returning from a trip to the latrines, or maybe from an overly long stay at the officers' club, had stumbled into a rain-filled slit trench. Inside every tent gales of spontaneous laughter would arise. It wasn't that we didn't feel a little sorry for the guy who'd wound up wet as a noodle in a soup bowl. We knew it was going to happen to somebody, and it almost always did.

Such was the rough humor in which we found refuge. It conveyed no malice, but it rounded out our lives. Deep down, we were proud of the accomplishments of our colleagues, individually and collectively. In that strange mix of fact and myth that forms all our perceptions and tempts our imaginations, we guys in the Flying Circus were developing our own *esprit de corps*.

On display now in group headquarters were letters of specific commendation to the group from generals MacArthur and Kenney, and from the commander of the Australian forces. And, of course, the presidential unit citation for our work over Balikpapan was the property of the whole 380th. It was something we could each feel we owned a small piece of.

Our enemies, too, had grown keenly aware of our group. Five times our base at Fenton had been visited by bombing raids. Once a force of thirty Japanese bombers destroyed three of our planes on the ground. A newly installed Australian anti-aircraft battery at Fenton knocked one of them out of the sky, and we got an up close look at its wreckage.

IN THE SECOND AND THIRD weeks of September, our squadron lost two crews. Their fates, though not immediately known to us, reflected the growing phobia our South Pacific foe nurtured toward our group. On the evening of September 11, David Lippencott's crew took off on a night mission to Makassar. Their goal was to destroy a 6,000-ton freighter anchored in the harbor. Pilot Lippencott and bombardier Hal Grace had been practicing a technique of low-level skip-bombing. Now, on that crew's seventeenth mission, they were eager to test their new skill against the real enemy.

Over the target, their plane ran into an intense volume of anti-aircraft fire. A violent explosion at low level over the water, seen by other crews, sent the bomber crashing into the ocean just beyond the wharf. That crash took the lives of all but four of the crew. The Japanese, we would later learn, seized these four survivors and subjected them to several days of physical beatings and abusive interrogations. The brutal facts were revealed by a group of Australian

POWs, who were forced to witness the ultimate fates of our colleagues. Their captors marched them, manacled and blindfolded, to the village square. There, as the other closely guarded prisoners watched in horror, the Japanese commander, wielding a large sword, ceremonially beheaded the four American air crewmen.

While stories of atrocity and barbarism committed by Japanese forces against captured prisoners were rife, this incident suddenly rose in our minds to an entirely different dimension of agony and outrage. This had happened to good friends of ours, and that made a difference.

The loss of his comrades was particularly hard on Lieutenant Joe Vick, the crew's original copilot who had been practicing to take over a crew of his own. Vick was replaced for this mission by a Minnesotan named Loyd Swan. My wife, Mab, had maintained correspondence with Swan's wife during this time of our absence.

TEN DAYS LATER, on September 21, our own crew's copilot, Bob Russell, agreed to fill a temporary vacancy on Wilbur Morris's crew for a mission to bomb the airdrome at Langgoer. Morris, his bombardier Paul Stansbury, and navigator Eddie Skuzinski occupied the tent next to ours. They were a tall, impressive-looking trio, Wilbur at six-three, Paul at six-two, Eddie at six-one. A lively friendship had developed between our two crews. It was Eddie's twenty-sixth birthday, and Paul's would come two days later. The two set plans for a joint celebration at the Bamboo Club, as we'd dubbed our officers' recreational shack, upon completion of the Langgoer mission.

Squadron Commander Jack Bratton led nine bombers—seven from the 530th and two from the 528th—in the raid. They encountered fierce aerial resistance from twenty to twenty-four Japanese army and navy interceptors, according to returning crewmen. A twin-engined Japanese fighter called a Nick, armed with a 37-millimeter cannon, scored a direct hit on Wilbur Morris's plane, ripping a huge hole in the right wing and starting a fire in the outboard number-four engine. Unable to keep the damaged aircraft steady or maintain altitude, Morris and Bob Russell were forced to crash-land the burning B-24 on a coral reef just offshore.

Several were hurt when the structure of the plane broke upon impact. The top turret was torn completely loose. Three were trapped, unable to extricate themselves from the wreckage. Eddie Skuzinski's back was broken, as well as both of his legs. His friends, having worked the others free, were trying desperately to pull Eddie loose from the wreckage when the Japanese boat patrol arrived to take them all into custody. Our crew tried to enlist their captors' help in pulling Eddie out of the foundered plane, but the naval patrolmen refused, forcing the ambulatory ones into life rafts at gunpoint, and then coldly abandoning poor Eddie, on his twenty-sixth birthday, to drown in the incoming tide.

The others became prisoners of war and survived. I would enjoy several pleasant reunions with Paul Stansbury in later years, and renew contact with Bob Russell. Yet I cannot forget Eddie, nor the eleven with Lippencott. When anyone speaks of the "glories" of war, I instinctively recoil. Sherman was right. War is hell. And the only way around it was right straight through it.

# 19

## LEADERSHIP, LUCK, AND A TASTE OF LEISURE

IT WAS MIDFALL, I GUESS—though I could be mistaken as to the exact time—when Col. Miller elevated Jack Bratton to group operations officer and Gus Connery became commander of the 530th. This meant a few extra duties, but not too many, for Pat Mullins as squadron navigator and for me as squadron bombardier. In truth, it probably was more title than trouble. Sensing maybe that I'd enjoy a little extra responsibility, Gus asked me to take on an additional job. With the loss of several crews, we began receiving replacements from U.S. training cadres. The pilots and crews were new to the region, unseasoned in combat, and unfamiliar with living and working arrangements, or even where things were at Fenton. Gus appointed me to meet and indoctrinate all the new crews in the ways and wonders of the 380th, what was expected of us, where to find things, who was who in the local pecking order, whom to consult for what kinds of problems—even down to such mundane stuff as what brands of Aussie whiskey to beware of. No extra pay, but what the heck? I had been promoted to first lieutenant.

Gus Connery was my mentor and my notion of one rock-solid, quality guy. He almost never blew his stack. And his judgment was sound. Gus seemed to understand the other person and how, in an easygoing way, to get the best out of his compatriots. It was, in a word, "leadership."

A particular case in point involved Joe Vick, a pilot from Chicago. Joe had come over as a second lieutenant and copilot for Dave Lippencott on *The Red Ass*. Like several other copilots, including our own Bob Russell and Loyd Swan who had flown in Vick's seat on that crew's last fatal mission, Joe wanted to become a senior pilot so he could manage a crew of his own.

Gus, like Bratton before him, insisted that the transition be preceded by a regime of special training and testing. Copilots seeking upward mobility would fly a course of noncombat training missions in the left-hand seat, abetted by a skeleton crew.

It was on one such mission, accompanied by no less than Col. Miller, that Joe endured his most harrowing experience. The B-24 Lt. Vick was flying hit a tree at the end of the runway on final approach, crippling the landing gear. The apparatus failed to lock and collapsed at impact with the runway, much like a knee that gives way and can't bear weight. The big plane hit with a thud, the underbody screeching and scronching down the runway and, finally, off the apron onto the reddish clay that ran alongside. Joe Vick struggled to control the runaway motion by determined foot pressure on the rudders, but the nose burrowed down into the ground as it finally came to rest.

Four passengers were killed on impact, and Col. Miller suffered a broken arm. The escape hatch below the pilot's compartment was sealed off when the front end of the plane dug into the earth. The exit door stuck, incapacitated by the ground pressures that inhibited its movement. Inside was Joe, bruised and slightly dazed from the collision of his head with the aircraft's solid superstructure. This condition was suddenly compounded by Joe's frustration at being trapped, unable to open the exit door, and by the pervasive fear that a gas tank might explode at any moment from the hot friction of the metal's long slide across the runway. It would have been enough to panic any but the most stoic personality.

Outside, Connery and a group of ground crewmen picked and dug frantically at the impacted earth with shovels, Gus all the while talking through the din to the trapped Vick, trying to soothe him, assure him, calm him. Luckily, the plane did not erupt in flames. Col. Miller and the other survivors cleared the wreckage through the bomb bay. When the rescue crew outside finally cleared the trapped and injured Lt. Vick, he was in a state of physical and nervous shock.

Gus was eager in the following days to get Joe on his feet and back in the cockpit as soon as possible. He visited the shaken pilot more than once in the field infirmary. As quickly as he was released, there was Captain Connery urging Joe Vick to come and fly with him.

At first Vick resisted. He'd been badly shaken by the experience and asked to be relieved from flying status. Gus would have none of it. "Nonsense, Joe, you're too good a pilot to lose." Joe felt guilty, haunted by the accidental scrape with the tree and his inability to keep the crippled plane on the runway, by what had happened to four of the passengers—and what would have befallen all if the craft had ignited. "You did all you could," Connery would persist. "The landing-gear failure was not your fault. It could have happened to anyone. Nobody could have handled that crisis better than you did!"

This went on for several days. Aware of Joe's apprehensions, I confronted Connery privately. "Why don't you back off, Gus? Joe's been through a hell of an experience. You need to give him a little time."

Gus smiled ruefully. "What is it you Texans always say? 'Get back on the horse that threw you?' The quicker I get Joe back in that cockpit, the sooner he'll get his confidence back. And the sooner that happens, the better off he'll be personally. I'm not just interested in salvaging *a pilot*. I want to save *Joe Vick*!"

That made sense. I hadn't thought about it that way. But Gus had.

He and Joe went up together, finally. Just the two of them at first. This went on for several more days. Then, Gus would invite Joe to fly occasionally as copilot with our crew. Finally, Joe commanded his own ship.

Bob Russell, our original copilot, had been training, likewise, to be a flight crew commander, going through the transitional routine, when he flew to Langgoer with Wilbur Morris's crew. He'd flown a combat mission from time to time with other command pilots, honing his own skills by observing how they handled moments of airborne crisis. Bob no doubt would have become a command pilot and had his own crew if he hadn't become a prisoner of war. (He was liberated at war's end and would reunite with Gus Connery briefly while both served, in the immediate postwar period, as pilots for Eastern Airlines.)

IT WAS OCTOBER. We had completed our twentieth bombing mission, and orders were cut awarding us a week of rest and relaxation. Col. Miller adhered to a general policy of an R&R week in some southern Australian city for every ten completed combat missions. We'd had a fine week in Adelaide back in late summer, and now eagerly looked forward to a second.

Our crew would be flown there and back in an Army C-47. The "Gooney Bird," as we called it, was the workhorse of the U.S. fleet. It was durable, easy to fly—and also, facing a stiff headwind that day, almost as slow as cold sorghum molasses. We stopped once, about halfway, in Alice Springs to refuel, commenting how lucky we'd be—considering the snail's-pace speed of our flight—if the week off didn't start 'til we got there.

When we'd earlier been to Adelaide, sometime in late August, I think, it was South Australia's winter. We were surprised at the severity of the civilian fuel shortage to which Australians disciplined themselves for sake of the war effort. Taxis, denied gasoline, were operating on charcoal burners attached to the vehicles' rear. The South Australian Hotel, Adelaide's best, dispatched the winter's chill by burning mallee roots in the lobby's open wood-burning fireplace. There was no central heating in the guest rooms, but the beds were big and warm blankets abundant. Their comfort was a welcome luxury after months of sleeping on army cots.

Not that we had any complaints. Compared with American infantrymen who'd be invading Europe within a year, we lived like royalty. When our actions caused death, as surely they did, we didn't have to suffer the visual human consequences. I sometimes wondered how I could have maintained a stable mental outlook if I'd been engaged in hand-to-hand combat, seeing the dead and dying up close—having to watch the contortion of a victim's face or hear his dying gasp as you stabbed him with your bayonet. And often not knowing from one day to the next where—or if—we'd be sleeping that night. Ours was, for all its tensions and pressures, a blissful disconnect from some of the hardships suffered by ground combatants.

On that earlier trip, our crew had watched an Australian football game, gone to a boxing match, twice visited the equivalent of the USO, played golf, and seen the city. A beautiful town it was, with a wide green belt of parkland and playgrounds between the downtown and the surrounding residential areas.

Unmarried men among us had met and dated Aussie girls. U.S. Army medics kept a list of young women who'd volunteered hospitality, and were considered responsible and free of communicable disease. Troops were not legally restricted to that list, but army doctors recommended it as a reference.

Now, in the convoluted springtime that comes to Australia in October, we were in for some new sights and different experiences. We spent one afternoon at the horse races, another at the ocean. Feeling great, I swam out to a big ship that I judged to be a quarter of a mile or so offshore. Swimming out was easy.

Only when I reached the ship and headed back toward the beach did I realize my mental omission of one crucial factor. The tide was going out, powerfully, as I began straining to swim in. Moreover, I'd misjudged the distance. The ship's great bulk had made it seem much closer to shore than it actually was. I realized this now with a start, seeing how tiny appeared all the figures on shore.

Out there alone in the big, blue Pacific, I had the disquieting sensation of drifting two strokes backward for every three strokes forward. Tiring, I dared not stop and tread water for fear of losing such hard-won progress as I'd made. Finally, after what seemed a week's work, physically drained, lungs bursting and shoulder sinews burning, I reached the shallow water and trudged through the retreating waves to the sandy shore. There I joined a group of American GIs who were trying to impress a half-dozen Aussie chicks, and stretched out beside them on the sand. Gulping air and only half listening, I offered no contribution to the conversation. I was completely out of breath, and the only things I had to say might have been to God. My mind was a jumble of vast relief, gratitude, and self-criticism.

What a sad sack of stuff, I thought, what a freak of cosmic irony, what a vacuum of meaninglessness, if I'd come safely through twenty combat missions and a dozen Jap bombings, with people shooting at me from over, under, and sidewise, only to drown un-seen somewhere in the big dumb ocean because I'd been too stupid to think about the tide.

That evening, Gus, Pat, Kelly, Johnny Tackett, and I stopped in at the official USO-type dance. There were easily twice as many American GIs in town as there'd been two months before. Everyone was having a loud, easy, laughing, talkative time. The band was playing music straight out of past Hit Parades. The hostesses were gracious, the girls friendly. Most liked to jitterbug, and those who couldn't wanted to learn. The crumpets and scones were tasty, the punch refreshing and harmless.

The Australian band, after an obligatory rendition of "White Cliffs of Dover," honed in enthusiastically on "Apple Blossom Time," while three Aussie girls did a fair imitation of the Andrews Sisters. My big mistake was always listening to the words of a song, and this one, even when imperfectly rendered, always made me nostalgic. I was glad to get off the dance floor. The young women were mostly both decorous and decorative, and that may have been part of the problem.

When the musicians took off with "Beer Barrel Polka," my mood lifted and I was easily lured back into the action. I liked polkas, perhaps because they demanded more athleticism than grace. But then, with a mellow sax leading the way, the ensemble shifted musical gears into a light, lilting version of "Moonlight Cocktail." That one always reminded me of a special evening in Galveston, that summer before Pearl Harbor, when Mab and I sat together in my borrowed car on the beach spinning dreams and watching moonlight on the water until the tires sank into the moistened sand, and I had an almost impossible time pushing it to safety as she steered it. We'd had a lot of laughs later, remembering the experience.

Now, the memory of it in my current situation made me feel vaguely uncomfortable. Mab at home, ten thousand miles away. The Aussie troops off in North Africa somewhere. After a little while, four of us—Gus, Pat, Kelly, and I—went out to dinner. Johnny had met a girl and wanted to stay longer. That night at dinner, back at the hotel, we discovered sparkling burgundy, and I wondered where it had been hiding all these years.

THE NEXT DAY was Sunday. I got up wanting to go to church. Pat and Gus had left for early mass by the time I got shaved, my tie-and-jacket uniform on and downstairs. In the lobby I ran into Mary Connelly, a prim little middle-aged Scottish spinster lady with shiny-clean white hair and thick remnants of what I supposed was a Highland brogue. Miss Connelly (she was too dignified and formal to call her Mary) served as head housekeeper for the hotel. This morning she was dressed in her Sunday best. She spoke cheerfully and asked if I wished to accompany her to church. She'd guessed me for a Presbyterian, she said, and that was right, though I considered myself ecumenical enough to feel at home in just about any worship service.

The minister was like so many of the Scottish-trained clergy, erudite and eloquent. Maybe they're the Jesuits of Protestantism. But his homily was down to earth. He addressed the human hardships of our besieged allies-in-arms, the Chinese. The preacher's effort was part of a church-wide mission, he said, to benefit the homeless, the hungry, the Chinese victims of military aggression, ruinous inflation, crop failures, and endemic disease. He wasn't asking for Bibles or ecclesiastical materials but for food and seeds and medicine. That preacher was so persuasive he almost made me ashamed of having no more cash than I had to drop in the collection plate!

After church, I joined some of the congregation as their guest for Sunday dinner. I'd wanted to get back and link up with my buddies, but the invitation was so insistent I felt I'd offend the hosts if I refused. Not content to empty their pockets for the poor Chinese, they wanted to do something for a visiting Yank. They treated me like a long-lost cousin.

On Monday, several of our crew went to visit a local winery. It had been recommended as a colorful and interesting experience. It was both. Springtime had brought new verdure to the vineyards that sprawled across the rolling terrain. The owner-manager welcomed us personally to his hospitality rooms, passed around glasses of three different shapes, and began to ply us with sipping samples from the best vintage years of his sundry types. None of us knew a darn thing about savoring the fragrance or lolling a bit of the mellow liquid on the tongue for its olfactory effect. Most of us probably supposed that "sipping" meant no more than just not chug-a-lugging a glassful down in one gulp. We were offered three reds, two whites, and one rosé, as I recall.

If our unsophisticated sampling techniques did not betray us, our crude efforts at complimentary commentary probably did. "Mighty good guzzlin', Sir!" is one cheerful comment that returns to mind. Our host showed no outward signs, however, of mistaking us for anything other than practiced connoisseurs. We probably stayed too long. I guess Gus, who never drank anything anyway, was the one who finally began making polite suggestions that we really must be going.

The next morning as we headed out to the airport to board our C-47 for its return to Fenton, I noticed a couple of fellows looked slightly blurry-eyed. Sergeant Farley, who in his career had served stints as a bartender and a medical corpsman, told us he was suffering from an ancient malady. He named it "The Wrath of Grapes." We all laughed as heartily as our respective conditions permitted. I remember thinking that was damn clever of Tom. I've heard that quip twice more, I think, in all the intervening years. Who knows, considering the way jokes get around, fade away, and are resurrected? Steinbeck's book hadn't been out but about three years or so at the time. Maybe Farley even invented that appropriate rearrangement of its title.

All in all, we were ready to get back to work. We'd been relaxing very strenuously.

# 20

## MAIL CALL, MESS HALL, AND EGG IN MY BEER

BACK AT FENTON, between missions, Pat Mullins and I played a private game as we met incoming crews, new to the outback and new to the war. Like other proud organizations, the Army Air Corps had spawned certain vanities and affectations of our own. There was a kind of distinctive swagger to the uniform—the gray trousers called "pinks" and forest-green jackets, as well as the massive tan shortcoats we wore back home in winter.

As a distinctive badge of our profession, flying officers took unspoken pride in removing the circular grommets from the crowns of what were called our "Garrison" hats. The rationale was practical if using the hat when flying, of course, as we attached earphones over our heads for intercom purposes while on missions. But the sartorial effect of floppy-crowned headgear was intentional in off-duty hours as an expression of professional pride, and tolerated widely even though unauthorized by dress regulations. A flying officer's fondest hope might be to sport a "thousand-hour hat" someday, worn ever-so-casually, back in the USA.

Mullins had a mischievous eye for human affectation of any sort. I'd first noticed this back in the States one day when he and I were leaving the base for a quick trip into town. "My God, Jim, you'll go blind," Pat exclaimed in mock horror. "Not to mention you're out of uniform. You forgot your dark glasses!" Among the unknowing targets of Pat's random ridicule were those of our flying colleagues who wouldn't be seen in public without the big wire-rimmed dark Ray-Ban sunglasses that were so popular those days among Army Air Corpsmen.

Now, after four or five months of flying out of Fenton, we had developed our own smug, petty conceits along with the casual lifestyle that befitted the Northern Territory's climate. New crews would disembark after their flight out from one of Australia's cooler southern cities, still dressed in their pinks and greens, or some wearing the big fleece-lined flying boots we kept for warmth at high altitudes. Pat would whisper, "Look, Jim. Intrepid airmen!"

Pat would pick out some natty newcomer with a parachute-silk scarf hanging around his neck and wonder, tongue in cheek, "whether the guy sleeps in that darn thing." Or, more likely, he might lure me into a bet about how many days it would be before some particular dandy-looking recruit would be running around camp in his T-shirt.

But these comments were kept to ourselves. There was no hazing. We knew only too well the uncertainties the newcomers felt beneath that exterior bravado. It was our job to make them feel comfortable, and welcome, and to give them every helpful piece of knowledge that we could. We may be counting on that very crew to protect our wing one day next week.

SOME OF US ENHANCED the quality of camp life by adopting pets. Soon after we'd arrived, maybe sometime back in May, we four tentmates had picked up two puppies, blue Australian cattle dogs. We called them "Smoky" and "Raunchy." They were great companions. The former took up with Gus and went everywhere with the captain in the squadron jeep Gus sometimes commandeered. The other pup took to following me around, until one night when he was run over by a truck scurrying to find cover during one of the air raids on Fenton.

Later, we inherited two cocker spaniels when their masters' crew was shot down. Duke and Mickey, as they were called, belonged to Wilbur Morris and Paul Stansbury, our tent neighbors. When their crew (including Bob Russell) became POWs, Pat and I became foster custodians for the two little cockers.

Behind us toward the baseball field lived a fellow from Denver named Leonard Wolfe. Leonard had bought two greyhounds off the racetrack while on rest leave. When the grass grew high after the rains had passed, these two sleek monsters would bed down out of sight beside the trail that led to the showers and pounce out suddenly, in the very path of some unsuspecting airman en route with little more than a towel, a bar of soap, and a pair of shoes. Despite repeated threats and entreaties, Wolfe took refuge in man's right to canine companionship, insisting the dogs were harmless. They never actually attacked anyone, and nobody died of a heart seizure. Ours was a fairly relaxed lifestyle, with minimal restraints.

Once while there, I committed the folly of buying a horse. Our Aussie friend, Bob Lea, told a few of us one day about a neighbor who had his Aborigine crew rounding up range horses for what seemed the equivalent of a spring roundup. Curious, we got directions and jeeped over to see the event.

I took a shine to a big sorrel. He stood almost sixteen hands high, I guessed, and had pretty good conformation, except too rangy for a show horse. Looking in his mouth, I judged him to be five, or maybe six years old. He was saddle-broke, but hadn't been ridden much. I bargained with the trail boss and bought him, on the spot, for twelve quid, which was close to forty dollars, with a used saddle and bridle thrown in. I called him "Mate," the term of collegiality most used by the Aussies.

The first thing Mate did when I got on him to ride him back to our camp was to brush up forcefully against a tree, trying to scrape me off. This called for laughter among the wiry Aborigines. That horse had a tough mouth, but I got him to behave pretty well on the three-mile trip back. We hobbled him while a couple of others and I built a corral out of tree posts and bamboo. It was sturdy enough, but primitive.

Then I rode him every day for a week, except once when the crew flew a mission. I'd haul big buckets of water and keep him in a shady place. The only trouble was feed. The quartermaster had nothing, and of course there were no stores or livery stables. With conspiratorial concurrence of a friendly cook, I "borrowed" some large boxes of oatmeal rations.

But it soon was unarguably apparent that I'd bitten off too much. I was staking Mate out to graze, scouting for lush pastures, carrying water, and wearing myself out. I doubt that Mate appreciated all these efforts on his behalf. He'd stare at me balefully through sorrowful eyes. In an unspoken prelude to that Crosby song that would be popular a year later, the message in the dumb brute's eyes was clear: "Don't Fence Me In!"

It was fall, the Australian springtime. The recently watered grass was high, and water stood fresh and clear in the billabongs. So I led him out of the corral, unbridled him, and gave him a sound swat on the rump. "Give it a go, Mate!" I shouted in his ear.

Mate cantered off, happy as a parade horse, in search of his herd.

THE FOUR TENT VILLAGES that served as home to our four squadrons, each with 150 or so inhabitants, gave us a tenuous hold on stability. We in the Air Corps were fortunate. Unlike the ground combat forces, whose ever-transient location shifted sometimes daily with the moving tides of war, we could sink at least shallow roots. Our tents would be there tomorrow and tomorrow, our foot-lockers under our cots holding little treasures of our individuality. Still, we never could lose sight of the common purpose that had brought us there. These places where we lived and worked and slept were, after all, company towns.

As with military personnel everywhere, Mail Call was the high-light of our week. Retreating into cocoons of privacy, we'd savor and reread almost any letter from home until we could have recited its text verbatim. Dad would write of humorous occurrences. My wife's letters were sentimental. She had begun helping Frances Gilbert, wife of my next-door neighbor, in operating that family's little cloth-ing store while Joe was away in the navy. My mother, I learned, had formed a ritual of slipping on my old suede jacket in the cool of the evenings, wearing it like a talisman. The younger of my two sisters, Betty Lee, was taking piano lessons and told me she'd mastered not only "Wild Blue Yonder," the Air Corps tune, but also "Sixpence," which I'd sung to her on my last leave home. Our middle sister, Mary Nelle, was a junior in high school. She kept sending me poems she had written—some funny, some philosophical.

Much has been written about the awful boredom of servicemen between combat engagements. I never felt it. I guess a typical crew was averaging a bombing mission about every fourth or fifth day. It sometimes took half a day to get ready and a full day to unwind from the tensions of a bombing raid over a defended target. And the ground maintenance crews needed a decent interval to test, check, and properly repair each of the aircraft's moving parts. They, the ground crews, were the unsung heroes who developed a love for the given plane to which they were assigned. To devoted mainte-nance guys, many of we flight crews owed our lives.

For me, in the days between missions, there was always some-thing interesting to do. Aside from my jolly duties as athletic offi-cer and official greeter of new crews, I cultivated a patch of land downstream from the shower stalls and got the squadron comman-der's permission to dig irrigation ditches for a modest garden, where a couple of colleagues and I harvested enough fresh tomatoes to share among appreciative airmen. I also devoured a lot of current books that season when duties permitted moments of solitude. My footlocker began to resemble a lending library. No time left for boredom.

Second only to Mail Call, the most popular institution of our village surely had to be the squadron mess hall. For all the grumbling about the food, nobody threatened to boycott the mess. Most of the fresh vegetables, when we could get them, were acquired from a large farm north of Fenton owned by our friend, Australian planter Bob Lea. I had several good conversations with this rugged fellow, and got a pointer or two for my tomato patch. The chefs, after a few months, were well experienced in mixing pancake batter. It seemed that was their primary breakfast skill.

The only alternative on most mornings was cold-storage eggs, scrambled. Bob Lea told me, when I asked why he didn't ever sell us some fresh eggs, that he reckoned there weren't enough hens in the whole Northern Territory to feed our crowd. Then, of course, there were the big containers of oatmeal, if you didn't mind washing it down with powdered milk. But, for all of that, I'll bet we ate as well, consistently, as any on-line combat outfit outside of England.

A ground sergeant had volunteered for tending bar at the Bamboo Club, as we'd informally named the 530th officers' recreational building. One day the sergeant, who'd worked with my volunteer cadre putting up the outdoor movie theater, confided that he'd bartered an Aussie out of some real, honest-to-God, hen-laid eggs.

"How would you like an egg in your beer, Lieutenant?" he grinned conspiratorially. The prospect was intriguing. The very words formed a staple of Air Corps repartee. Egg in my beer! Whenever anyone expressed dissatisfaction with what fate had dealt him, someone would bring him down to earth with the popular rejoinder, "Whaddya expect? Egg in your beer?"

So now I was offered an actual chance to sample that optimum delicacy! Wondering what it could be like, I said "Sure, why not?" I checked out one of the two tall bottles of heavy Australian beer which were the weekly ration for each airman and poured it slowly into a big glass. I filled the glass almost full, careful to leave just enough room for the egg. The sergeant proudly reached into a corner of the big refrigerator where he had sequestered the prize egg.

He held it gingerly, cracked it ever so easily on the glass's rim. Deftly pulling the halves apart, he let the contents slide into my glass.

Observers standing around to witness this ceremony gasped. Some swore profanely. The sergeant's face was a mask of horror, as malodorous fumes rose to our nostrils.

The egg was rotten!

The horrified reactions, the looks on their faces, struck my funny bone. I laughed out loud. That seemed to pierce the gloom. But now I realized I'd squandered half my beer ration for the week. Then I remembered something my dad always said by way of consolation. "You can't win 'em all!" And that's what I said, to the observable relief of the visibly shaken sergeant. He'd tried, after all, to do me a big favor.

ONE DAY A LETTER from Mab brought a jolt. Disbelieving, I read it a second time. My head spun, and my eyes wouldn't focus. My best friend in college, the words were saying, had been killed. The message was straightforward enough. Why was it so hard to accept? Lieutenant Harold Owen, recently commissioned pilot, had been killed in the line of duty when his P-38 went down during a high-altitude training mission. That was it. I didn't believe it, didn't want to believe it.

Without a word, I walked out of the tent, down the road, past the end of our village, across a broad, open meadow and through a big clump of trees, with no intentional destination. I kept walking, waiting for my mind to clear. *Harold.* He and I had put out the college newspaper together. We'd been debate colleagues for two semesters. Together, in the spring of '41 we'd bought a 1931 Model A Ford coupe for $50. Together. We'd both signed the note at the bank. We'd sold the car six months later for $55.

*Harold.* One night two years ago, five of us had been ready to go to Canada and join the Royal Canadian Air Force. The next day Harold and I had sobered up. The other three went. Johnny and Charlie Botvidson and Billy Wayne Maddox. Now two of our friends were majors, and maybe even lieutenant colonels by now. And Harold was dead. *Dead?* This wasn't supposed to happen. I always thought he'd be governor of Texas someday. Or publish the state's most influential daily. Or something. Not die. Not get killed.

Finally, I accepted it. It was fact. Cruel, damn fact. That's all. Just like Corpening and Stoner and all their crew. Just like the guys on our wing on that first mission to Timor. Just like Loyd Swan, and Eddie Skuzinski on his twenty-sixth birthday. Like all the rest of the good guys who'd died. Damn war! I don't know how long I walked, but my mind closed onto the grimy, immutable facts.

It was dinnertime. I remember now how Bob Russell and Loyd Swan had always sat at a back table in our mess hall talking between themselves, long after all the rest of us had finished eating and left. I went into the mess hall, got some food and a mug of coffee, went over to that back table, and sat in the empty space they'd left. I felt better.

Egg in my beer. That's what it was, egg in my beer. What did I expect? Things would work out. We'd defeat the Japanese, and the Germans, and all get to go home. It just took time. We had to be making progress. There were rumors that we might go over to New Guinea. Things were closing in on the Japanese. We could feel it.

# 21

## HITS AND MISSES, HIGH AND LOW

MILITARY CRITICS WRITING in the twenty-first century, acquainted with the fiendish accuracy of laser-guided missiles and other modern precision weaponry, might look upon World War II's state-of-the-art equipment as downright primitive.

One can read some startling statistics. We are told, for example, that the United States, in only five or six *weeks* of active bombardment against Iraqi targets during the Persian Gulf War in 1991, actually rained down a greater tonnage of deadly explosives upon the forces of that one nation, Iraq, than *all* the military powers dropped upon *all* enemy targets, in *all* the theaters of war during *all the years* of World War II.

Incredible? Yes, but reportedly accurate. Some other modern assessments, measuring our 1940s performance by rough circular bombing error, have written that the average aerial bomb dropped in World War II missed its target by about half a mile. This could be correct, but I can't believe it. Based upon my own limited observation, I'm inclined to question it. At the risk of being accused of remembering selectively, I do think we did, on average, a good bit better than that.

This is not to say that we didn't miss the mark sometimes. Of course, we did. My only claim to any celebrity in the group, I think, was in having placed the first bombs on Balikpapan. This is the way I was sometimes introduced to new crews joining our group as replacements. Mighty small claim to fame. Yet, any celebrity is better than none, and I secretly ate it up! Better than good sorghum molasses on a homemade biscuit.

But my pride was fairly short-lived. Only a few weeks after I'd succeeded to the more or less honorary title of squadron bombardier, our crew was flying a two-plane reconnaissance mission over the Flores Sea, along with that of Major Jack Bratton and "Porky" McFerrin, my predecessor in the "squadron bombardier" title.

Someone spotted a large, presumably loaded merchant vessel, steaming in an easterly direction in the waters between Soemba, Soembawa, and the western end of Flores Island. This was in November or December, a time when we were consciously striving to dry up the shipping lanes link of Japanese ammunition and supply replenishments. What a juicy target, apparently loaded with the wares we now were intent on denying our foe.

Each of the two planes made a run at an altitude of about 6,000 feet, crossing the ship's line of movement at roughly a 45-degree angle. We each carried six bombs, and each plane dropped a train of three at this altitude.

McFerrin's overshot the target; mine undershot it and were off slightly to the right of its wake, churning up the sea but missing the ship.

Chagrined at our poor aim, the two premier squadron command pilots of the 530th, and we who'd been held up as ace bombardiers, agreed on a low-level attack, on the deck. Circling and regrouping for a new chance at the promising target, we began our run at probably 200 feet. McFerrin and I were to wait until we could discern the clear shape of a human body aboard the vessel and, then, each to toggle his remaining three bombs. This time, we were flying perpendicularly across the ship's azimuth. We missed again. I had waited a split second too long. My first bomb hit the water about 100 feet before we crossed the vessel's hull, and the other two overshot it. Gunners on deck were firing at us.

Damn! Now we were out of bombs. Both crews. It was embarrassing to return to base and report having missed entirely. Twice! High level and low. But our people *had* to be alerted to this target of opportunity. Someone else—with better aim today, we bitterly acknowledged—must take off with bombs and track it down. Scorched earth. Sink the supplies. Starve out the Japs.

GUS AND I never really perfected the deadly knack of the low-level attack. Even in our scarce practice runs, we'd miss as often as we'd hit. The two bombing techniques were absolutely different, requiring different skills.

Overhead bombing was cerebral; low-level was intuitive—like firing a shotgun at a suddenly flushed covey of quails. Upper-level releases, using the bombsight and the right mathematical calculations, were scientific. Just releasing the bomb with your thumb on the toggle switch as you fly swiftly past the target requires more the talent of a gunslinger in a Wild West saloon.

There was something else, in my case, I think. The *sight* of the people you're getting ready to obliterate—up close—does something indefinable to you. I remember hunting trips as a youth, rites of passage. Scoring a hit on the wild turkey and seeing it fall brought a swift rush of momentary exaltation—but what followed almost immediately was a depressing cloud of regret. Why'd I have to do that, my mind would ask.

That mood fluctuation was still more pronounced with a deer. In those days in Texas, when boys were initiated into the rituals of hunting at fifteen or so, I never mentioned these emotions. They were too private. That feeling surely had to be magnified manifold times when one's victim was an identifiable human being.

Years later, I'd read a recognizable sentiment in William Manchester's sensitively written war memoir, *Goodbye, Darkness.* "One of my worst recollections," wrote the former marine, "one I had buried in my deepest memory bank long ago, comes back with a clarity so blinding that I . . . am appalled by it, filled with remorse and shame. I am remembering the first man I slew."

So much for misses. In some aspects, hits were worse. But this was war. And as some paratroopers in the 101st Airborne now celebrate in arm tattoos, *killing* was *our business*. It was the only way out of this grisly mess, and, as I reminded myself, I volunteered for it.

AN ENTIRELY DIFFERENT OUTLOOK on low-level attacks comes to light in an episode involving a lean and lanky, six-foot-four, quintessential Texan named Virgil Stevens who joined our outfit as a replacement pilot in the 529th.

"Big Steve," as he came to be known, arrived with a lot of previous stick experience. He was probably twenty-seven and had been flying since the age of seventeen. A native of Chillicothe, Texas, Steve had graduated from Central High School in Fort Worth and Santa Ana Junior College in California, where he went on a football scholarship. Once, following a game in which Steve had scored the only touchdown, the local newspaper's story contained one slight typographic error. Instead of referring to the star player as Virgil Stevens, the misprint listed him as *Virgin* Stevens. Steve registered this complaint with the editor: "You have either misspelled my name or published a factual inaccuracy."

Graduating from that institution, Steve, who'd already been flying for several years, applied for admission to the aviation cadet program, only to be rejected because of his size. U.S. military flight schools in those prewar days concentrated mainly on training pilots for fighter aircraft, with their more cramped cockpit space limitations. Steve's six-foot-four-inch frame automatically disqualified him.

So he'd gone to Canada and joined the Royal Canadian Air Force (RCAF), which imposed no such restrictions. After war came to us on December 7, the U.S. Air Corps relaxed that restraining height limitation, and Steve transferred over to join his own countrymen. By the time he came to us in the 380th he was a captain, and a highly experienced one.

In the 529th, Steve made a hit with his cohorts and was soon assigned as the squadron pilot training officer, given the task of breaking in several Australian pilots in the vagaries and idiosyncrasies of the B-24. This integration of U.S. and Aussie crew members in the same fighting units was an experiment unique to the Flying Circus. It was a project close to the heart of AVM Adrian Cole, whose brainchild it was. Big Steve and the Aussie pilots developed a rapport, and two of them frequently flew on his wings in the three-plane bombing formation.

Once, leading a six-plane flight to bomb newly built enemy airdromes on the island of Noemfoor—whose warplanes had been attacking U.S. ground forces—Stevens faced a critical decision. On his wings flew two planes piloted by his Australian pupils.

Knocking this airdrome out of commission promptly was essential. Enemy planes flying from this strip were harassing, disrupting, and endangering American ground troops currently fighting to establish a beachhead on Hollandia.

Twice, first at the scheduled 9,000-foot altitude, then at 4,000, bombs missed due to severe visibility problems. Drifting cloud banks covered the targets below. Having failed to score crippling damage, they were out of bombs, enemy warplanes still intact.

Unwilling to quit, and spotting a hole in the clouds, Steve restructured his six aircraft into a single-file formation for descent. Coming in low on the deck in a straight line following Steve's lead, they strafed the airdrome's vulnerable targets with machine-gun and cannon fire.

It was a bold, razzle-dazzle maneuver that pierced Japanese fuel tanks, setting aflame several enemy aircraft on the runway and blowing up an ammunition dump. The six-plane team returned to base, pleased and excited by their stunning exploit.

When they'd landed, parked their aircraft, and appeared for debriefing, however, they saw several ashen faces. "Steve," said one of the pilots still lingering in the debriefing room, "you're in trouble. Major Brissey swears he's going to court-martial you for disobeying orders!" Steve didn't see Major Brissey, the 529th commander, and just let matters rest for the night.

Just why Major Forrest Lee Brissey would have contemplated a court-martial is something of a puzzle. Brissey had been an important part of group leadership from the beginning, a squadron commander and group operations officer. By reputation, he was a stickler for regulations.

Brissey frowned on hot-dogging, or showy stunting. I believe both he and Col. Miller had expressed reservations against using the B-24 for strafing. That, they felt, was a job for fighter aircraft. Brissey had led a flight of six at 9,000 feet over the same overcast target slightly prior to Steve's. And it is quite likely that when he verbally threatened that court-martial action, Brissey was unaware of the low-level raid's results.

Totaling up the damage, intelligence officers were astonished: the six-plane raid, with incendiary tracer bullets, had set off several huge cans of aviation fuel that the Japanese had arranged protectively around the parked aircraft. In all, seventeen Japanese warplanes had been destroyed. The boys in the U.S. landing party on Hollandia would be happy.

So, it developed, was Australian Air Vice Marshal Cole. He telegraphed a strong, congratulatory message to the 529th, effusively praising the mission and the maneuver. He commended the strafing activities in particular, saying they "would have done credit to a fighter squadron."

Nothing more was said about a court-martial.

The Australian high command cited the Aussie pilots, John Napier and Richard Overheu, for their stellar participation, and Big Steve was awarded both a Distinguished Flying Cross and a Silver Star. Hero stuff!

But it isn't for medals that heroes dare. Nor praise nor fame nor abstract causes. William Manchester, who as earlier mentioned had seen much killing, wrote in *Goodbye, Darkness* that heroes die not for slogans but for their friends, for one another. I think there's truth in that.

## 22

### HERO STUFF

IT'S HARD TO DEFINE A HERO—just who is and who isn't one. It's a subjective standard, of course, and heroes exist, to a large extent, in the eyes of the beholder.

Most certainly it can be argued that anyone who gives his or her life in the service of our country is a hero. I'd not dispute that. Nor, in a broader sense, would I ever quarrel with a boy who tells me his father or mother is a hero.

Nobody among the guys I knew thought of himself as a hero. Had anyone claimed any such self-identification, he'd have been laughed out of camp. I do not, in fact, remember the word even coming up in conversation.

In the narrower context of just who qualifies as a national hero, particularly a national war hero, I suppose the requisites must be reasonably restrictive. John McCain has written an entire book aimed at defining courage. Some of those he cites as exemplars of that trait could well be considered heroes. An element of daring must be somehow implicit in a war hero's deeds. But being a hero is not synonymous with being foolhardy.

From the beginning of flight school, aviation cadets were indoctrinated in the maxim that *there are no old, bold pilots*. That primary, cautionary common wisdom is a time-tested starting place of aviation training.

Yet, wise and essential as are care and caution, some element of risk is inevitable. Risk is inherent in living, inseparable from war, omnipresent in combat. Wisdom lies in the ability to estimate the degree of risk and weigh it in the balance against the likelihood of success and the quantum of good that will be its reward.

More simply put: What are our chances, and is the prize worth it?

In war, everyone faces these decisions on one level or another. And, contrary to the absolute finality of the wonderfully worthwhile slogan, *no old, bold pilots*, it did and does have its exceptions. One such, in my estimation, was Virgil Stevens. He was bold, very bold, where exigencies demanded, but blissfully privileged, for all his hours of flying, to grow peacefully old before his dying.

Less lucky were some others. Two of our group's daring performers were John Farrington and Fred Hinze—the latter, the ebullient Lone Ranger who had, months earlier, drawn Col. Miller's censure for using a B-24 to dust the sagebrush and chase coyotes across the desert. Fred was a hot pilot. He was daring, yet not unmindful of the well-being of those sharing the risk with him.

The crews of these two pilots suffered cruelly, though bravely, one afternoon in late October, following a successful bombing raid in the Celebes. They had completed their bomb runs without interception, leaving the vital Japanese nickel processing plant at Pomelaa in a smoldering heap of rubble, and a 3,000-foot freighter in the harbor with a ruptured hull, its fuel supply aflame as it oozed out of its busted containers.

As the two Circus aircraft, their raid completed, fell into formation with three others for the flight back to Australia, the intercom crackled with warning. "Bandits at two o'clock!" A swarm of Zekes, belatedly alerted at their Kendari air base, began attacking the bomber formation.

The Japanese fighters, as if by prearrangement, seemed to concentrate their fire on the B-24 in the number-two slot. It was *Fyrtle*

*Myrtle*, piloted by John Farrington. On the third pass, that Liberator's nose guns fell silent and heavy smoke gushed up from the retracted nose-wheel compartment. An accurate burst of cannon fire had scored a direct hit on the nose section, killing bombardier John Perry and nose gunner Sergeant James DeGroat. The hydraulic system was fractured, and the heavy, claret-colored lubricant began to fill the crawl space between nose and flight deck.

After the next almost head-on pass, both pilot and copilot for *Fyrtle Myrtle* were wounded, and the number-two engine was ablaze. Farrington's wounds were so disabling that the copilot, Lieutenant Tracy DuMont, had to take over the controls. He was a replacement copilot, and this was his first actual combat mission in a B-24. Now he felt skin surface burns from an incendiary round, and shrapnel fragments had pierced his skin, but DuMont was physically able to handle the ship while Farrington, fatally wounded, muttered advice.

*Fyrtle Myrtle* clearly was in no shape to complete the return trip to base, and DuMont maneuvered the burning Liberator into a steep left-turning descent, hoping to reach a designated escape point on a nearby island where the remaining crew could bail out with a reasonable chance of help from local natives and a clandestine pickup by a PBY rescue plane.

The aircraft's damaged condition made it erratic to handle, however, and the billowing smoke from the nose fire filled the cockpit, obscuring sight of the instrument panel. Word went to the crew in the rear to bail out.

Fred Hinze and his crew in *Golden Gator*, breaking formation, followed the doomed and rapidly descending plane in an effort to protect its crew from annihilation by the swarming Zekes. In this, they succeeded, but only by diverting the Zeke pack's attention to themselves.

Parachutes opened, lifting crew members above the falling plane. With only the pilots and the two dead airmen aboard, *Fyrtle Myrtle* exploded in a great ball of fire just before hitting the water.

Miraculously, six *Fyrtle Myrtle* crew members managed to parachute to safety at water's edge, to hide themselves in the island's convolvulus flowering foliage until dark. The next morning they borrowed a boat from natives. Alas, the six were apprehended in their effort to escape in the small craft. They were taken into custody by a Japanese boat patrol and made prisoners of war. Still, they lived.

Had Fred Hinze and the *Golden Gator* crew not risked their own lives to distract the enemy Zeke pilots, these six survivors quite probably would have been cut to ribbons by relentless fire from the Zekes after escaping the burning plane and before reaching the safety of the island's shoreline.

The diversionary tactic that spared their lives, however, had attracted the full wrath of the six remaining Zekes to *Golden Gator*. One of them scored a direct hit on the number-four (the outer right) engine, from which flames began to spurt. Soon power went out in the number-one engine. The now underpowered Liberator was even more at the mercy of the attackers.

Luckily, Hinze found a billowy cloud formation in which to take temporary refuge. Once safely hidden, the crew was able to extinguish the burning engine's fire, but the B-24 was still underpowered, with both outer engines feathered and nonfunctional. Worse, it had lost contact with the other B-24s in the original formation.

Shortly after emerging from the cloud's protective cover, *Golden Gator* was again spotted by the prowling Japanese fighter pilots. Like a wolf pack chasing a wounded deer, and suddenly smelling blood, they set upon the injured and now slower prey with a fury. Soon the number-three engine began coughing and sputtering, damaged by incessant fire-spitting flybys.

Hinze, in an effort to restart the idled number-four engine, pushed the B-24 into a dive while "windmilling" the engine. He also wanted to give his plane's harassers less maneuvering room by seeking a very low altitude. *Golden Gator*'s underside actually scraped or collided with the top branches of a tall clump of trees on the lushly vegetated island. This damaged the propellers and made the task of stabilizing the plane and keeping it airborne ever more difficult.

The fleet of Zeke pilots, baffled by the big plane's ability to stay aloft at all, and probably themselves running out of ammunition and fuel after swift pursuit for more than an hour, broke off their chase and returned to base. *Golden Gator's* gunners had downed three or four, maybe more, of the interceptors.

The *Gator* had escaped its pursuers and was still flying, though with less power and more slowly. All of the crew were alive, and following the long, fierce running battle, only two had suffered wounds. After covering about three hundred more miles over the Flores Sea, the crew realized the need to jettison as much unneeded weight as possible if the crippled, underpowered Liberator was to have a shot at making it home.

There'd be one more chance of enemy interceptors over Timor. So they saved back a few rounds of ammunition for the top turret gunner, then dumped all excess weight—including empty fuel tanks and the remainder of the heavy guns and ammunition—overboard from the stressed-out plane. Three hours had passed since the encounters with the Zekes. The radio operator had been unable to get a response from Darwin.

Another problem arose as the cables holding the big, empty bomb racks refused to let go while the crew tried to salvo them into the sea through the open bomb bay doors. They dangled there, causing more drag as *Golden Gator* limped along only a few feet above the waves, its crew hoping to avoid detection.

Now Hinze and navigator Ed Green agreed that the plane, in this condition, could never reach the Australian coast. They decided the best hope of the crew's survival would be to ditch the plane on little Moa Island, off the coast of Timor. But more bad luck loomed ahead.

At 1903 hours (three minutes after 7 P.M.), two Nicks—apparently a flying patrol—spotted the big lumbering craft flying just over the waters approaching Moa.

Sergeant Johnny Wine, top turret gunner, fired bravely at the on-coming duo, using up the remaining ammunition. He stayed at his post until a bullet hit him squarely in the head, killing him instantly. There being no other defensive fire coming from *Gator*, the Japanese fighter pilots knew the plane was out of ammo and defenseless.

For seventeen minutes, the two fully loaded interceptors' guns had an undeterred field day, repeatedly spraying the bomber with intensive fire from every angle of approach. Tailgunner Robert Wolfe, waist gunner Howard Collett, nose gunner Mark Mitchell, and photographer Aldo Bottigleo all died from the withering machine-gun assaults.

Flying straightway into the oncoming B-24, shells from one of the Nicks exploded into the cockpit, one striking Fred Hinze in the face and blinding him in one eye. Copilot Francis Herres was struck in both legs, and another bullet destroyed his flight controls. Like Tracy DuMont, he was a converted A-20 pilot, flying his first B-24 mission.

With right side controls completely out of commission, Hinze, bleeding from his face wound, was forced to control the plane alone. Bombardier Bob Jones took a station between the two pilots and watched in horror as Fred Hinze's left foot was blown off. Jones applied a tight tourniquet to stanch the bleeding and felt fragments pierce his own body from another exploding round.

Through all of this, Fred Hinze—now half blind, bleeding profusely, and using only his right foot for both right and left rudders—relentlessly pursued his mission to land the plane safely on the island and thus give the remaining crew members their best possible chance of survival.

On the final leg of his ditching approach, one of the Nicks, in another head-on pass, fired a shell that struck Hinze squarely in the chest. Using his fast-waning last breath, the bold pilot successfully ditched the plane on solid ground without starting a fire. Literally within seconds, he was dead.

Flight engineer Bill Fansler manually released the life rafts. Copilot Herres, assisting in this effort, was struck down and killed by a bullet from a strafing pass. Fansler was hit but not fatally. He, Green, Statland and Jones quickly turned the rafts bottoms-up and hid underneath them.

On the next strafing run, both enemy pilots, seeing no survivors, must have concluded that everyone was dead. So satisfied, they flew away in the fast descending twilight.

After dark, the four surviving crewmen, lashing the two rafts together, launched them quietly into the water and drifted for two days, praying that someone had received their SOS distress messages and triggered a search for them.

Someone had. An Aussie PBY crew spotted them and brought them aboard, then safely back to their home base. Their firsthand story of the harrowing day, and the undeniable heroism that had spared their own lives, made the rounds.

So inspiring was it that the group officially nominated Fred Hinze for a posthumous Congressional Medal of Honor. For reasons unknown, that award was never finalized in Washington. The 380th never made any other nominations for this supreme honor, but we felt Fred, in saving the lives of colleagues while losing his own, had earned it.

That, when you come right down to it, is the stuff of heroes.

What irony! Fred Hinze, in the sober view of the leadership, was bad news, at times a pariah. Fred was a free spirit, an incurable nonconformist, "his own man." One popular term others had applied to Fred was "screwball."

He almost didn't even get to ship out with the group. Brissey wanted to leave Fred behind, and, after his third or fourth whimsical stunt in disregard of stated policy, Col. Miller was ready to drop Hinze from the roster.

Only upon the earnest intercession of Captain Jack Kelly, 529th operations officer, whom Bill Miller liked and trusted, did the group commander relent. "Let him fly over as my copilot," pleaded Kelly, "and I'll be responsible for him." Fred Hinze, after that, would have died for Jack Kelly. Maybe, in a sense, he did.

When the chips were down, the lives of his comrades almost literally dangling in the balance, Fred did the right and eminently courageous thing. In the face of death, he spent his last breath giving them a chance to live.

Try telling the survivors of those two crews that Fred Hinze was not a hero.

# 23

## UMBRELLA FOR MACARTHUR'S BOYS

TOWARD THE END OF OCTOBER and continuing through November, the Pacific War entered an entirely new phase, in which our own role was fundamentally changed. The Australian Command began integrating planes from the 380th, along with those of other units, into occasional strike-force operations. These were bigger bombing fleets than any we'd ever seen, attacking Japanese positions in New Guinea and on New Britain.

Sometimes we flew now alongside RAAF squadrons, sometimes with shorter-range American B-25 contingents, occasionally with fighter accompaniment. Smaller reconnaissance missions, meanwhile, were constantly being sent out to probe shipping lanes with the aim of sinking or crippling enemy troop carriers or merchant vessels headed for Japanese ports with reinforcements.

Something was up, and we thought we knew what it was. General Douglas MacArthur, supreme Allied commander for the Pacific, was using the air arm to soften up enemy defenses on New Britain and upper New Guinea for a massive invasion by Allied ground forces. Part of this was cutting off and drying up our foes' supply lines, starving them, if we could, of fuel and ammo replacements.

The main obstacle to fulfilling our objective was the weather. It was foul over our target areas and seemed to be deteriorating weekly. Rain in the New Guinea–New Britain sector was much more intense than in Northern Australia where we were based. We heard that the nasty drip, drip, drip in our Allied enclaves in southern New Guinea had already delayed construction of auxiliary landing strips to support the coming invasions. Now, the dismal strata of heavy rain clouds that darkened the skies down to very low altitudes, obliterating our view of targets, was giving the Japanese a reprieve and time to repair the damage our bombs were inflicting.

One day Jack Bratton, now a major, led a reconnaissance flight that spotted a convoy of smaller Japanese supply ships which had slipped in under cloud cover to the port at Sorong on New Guinea's northwest coast. Bratton's crew, along with those of Captain John Dennis and First Lieutenant Joe Vick, now a full crew commander, destroyed or sank almost the whole convoy.

Our persistent attacks apparently were taking their toll on the fleet of Japanese interceptor aircraft, as only one lone Zeke defender rose to contest them. Joe Vick must have felt that hard knocks would never quit hounding him. The single interceptor landed a solid 20-millimeter shot on his plane's right bomb bay, piercing the fuselage and wounding both waist gunners in the explosion.

All three Liberators returned safely. The two gunners were treated at the infirmary. Joe now found himself practicing on his gunnery crew the same reinforcing cajolery Gus had used only weeks earlier to massage him back into action. The gunners recovered and were soon back on duty. All in all, it had been a very productive mission.

Other days were less fruitful, extending into frustrating weeks. General MacArthur was determined to isolate and demolish Rabaul, our stubborn nemesis on New Britain's northeastern tip. Rabaul's neutralization was an essential objective if an Allied invasion of New Britain was to succeed without massive losses. Ninety aircraft, a joint mission and by far our biggest to date, included our 528th and 531st squadrons, along with some from the 43rd and 90th U.S. Bomb Groups, and others flown by the RAAF.

This huge bombing strike force, flying in loose formation, was to be joined at a rendezvous point about fifty miles out from target by an escort wing of sixty-five P-38s to attack and fight off interceptors. Maddeningly, the clouds and fog were as dense as pea soup. Visibility was zilch! Neither contingent could see anything at all.

Bomber and P-38 pilots, guiding by instruments, missed their rendezvous. All felt the constant stress, unable to see fifteen yards beyond their own wing tips, incessantly fearing a midair collision. At an estimated ten miles off Rabaul harbor, thick fog enshrouded the entire coastline with an impenetrable dark gray curtain. Dropping bombs would have been sheer guesswork. The mission was scrubbed, and everyone returned to base—tense, unfulfilled, and disgruntled, but vastly relieved to plant feet again on Mother Earth. Their one consolation was that, with that many aircraft moving in such close proximity, there'd been no collision.

ON NOVEMBER 27, the 380th observed its first birthday. Col. Miller declared a whole day off from flight duty for all personnel. This would be a day of celebration, mingling solemnity with fun, including intersquadron softball games. Exactly one year earlier, the group had come into formal being at Davis-Monthan Field, in Tucson, Arizona.

Some of us, still in flight schools on November 27, 1942, would join up in the ensuing month. I didn't graduate with my wings and commission until December 12. It had taken three or four weeks to assemble all the needed skills, get personnel selected, and assigned to crews.

Now, in only a little over six months of actual combat, our Flying Circus had set a new world distance record, won a presidential unit citation, racked up more than two hundred confirmed "kills" of enemy aircraft, and sunk or put out of commission more than sixty shipping vessels. We had "strategically wounded Japanese capabilities" in the region, we were told at an outdoor ceremony that day by AVM Adrian Cole, head of the Australian Command to which we reported. Cole answered directly to General George Kenney, and we answered to Cole. Both Aussie and American airmen referred to him informally as "King" Cole. He knew this and apparently didn't mind it.

But all those gains had exacted a mighty toll. The ceremony was a solemn memorial to our 154 air crewmen killed or missing in this fateful year. In these past six months, we'd lost 45 percent of our starting number. Some minds, hearing these figures, must have stopped to linger on the odds. Sadder yet, two of the *replacement* crews had already gone down. Our crew, not yet knowing Bob Russell was a prisoner of war, named him in our thoughts.

ON DECEMBER 9, all of our 529th and 530th crews, along with nine from the other two squadrons, were deployed to New Guinea. We'd be bivouacked on temporary duty at Dobodura, a miserable, rain-drenched base just east of the Owen Stanley mountain range. We learned that we'd be part of the all-out Allied effort to take New Britain and New Guinea. We would fly cover over coordinated ground troop landings, try to destroy the Japanese artillery positions dug in behind the landing beaches, and otherwise provide support for our troops coming ashore in landing craft.

We felt, on arriving at this big, newly thrown-together staging area, that we'd been put down on the edge of a swamp. Everything was drenched with rain, and the place smelled of mildew. Mosquitoes were rampant. They were, our medics told us, of the anopheles variety, carriers of malaria. We were advised to take a daily dose of Atabrine—the only available antidote, since the Japanese had overrun all the areas that produced quinine and our medical corps had long since exhausted its supplies. Permanent party troops at Dobodura bore the telltale signs of prolonged Atabrine usage: their skin had turned yellow.

Compared with the rustic comforts we'd come to call home at Fenton, Dobodura held several rude surprises. We found ourselves appreciating the degree to which we'd been spared some of the harsher inconveniences that were the regular lot of this permanent party at Dobodura.

For one thing, the territory had been more recently recaptured from the Japanese than Port Moresby, where some of us had landed once earlier. There still were little nests of snipers in the surrounding woods, we were told. They'd been abandoned there when the main Japanese force had pulled out, retreating to their new front lines north and west of this location. Two weeks earlier, we learned, a nest of three lonely holdouts was rooted out of the woods, hungry and out of ammunition. They were fed and put under guard, on a plane to Townsville for interrogation and, presumably, internment as prisoners of war.

Our living quarters were damp and dismal. The pyramidal tents to which we were assigned sagged from the soaking rains that collected in big, bucketful-size puddles on all sides of the concave sloping roofs. Anyone mistakenly jostling a tent from the outside could get drenched. Many did. The floors inside the tents, underneath the cots on which we slept, were constantly covered with at least two inches of water. We'd brought along our B-4 bags for a change of clothes, but after the third day of incessant rain, nobody had a dry garment left, and there was no sun under which to dry them.

The ground facilities and base personnel clearly hadn't been prepared for this sudden influx of crews. There wasn't any warm water, for example, in which to wash mess kits. After several days, an epidemic of dysentery spread among the crews, and this complicated things aloft as we carried out a demanding schedule of missions.

There were five main targets on New Britain: Cape Gloucester, Cape Hoskins, and Rabaul on the long northern coast facing the Bismarck Sea; Arawae and Gasmata on the island's southern side. Our thirty-four crews took off in muggy weather on December 13, hoping to destroy the landing field at Cape Hoskins. When we got there, a collection of cumulonimbus clouds containing active thunderstorms hovered directly above our target, making flying the bomb runs hazardous and rendering target visibility almost nil. So our formation turned south across the island and unloaded our bombs on a coastal area near a planned beachhead of our eminent invasion.

The next day, ten of our crews struck a target on the Arawae peninsula in the morning. In a second raid that afternoon, the same crews returned to hit another site in the same vicinity. Both targets lay within that segment of the southern coast where our 112th Cavalry Regiment was scheduled to storm ashore early the next morning.

Every crew in the strike force with a combat-ready plane flew two missions that day. In all, we pounded that string of coastal defenses with 433 tons of explosives. The U.S. cavalry regiment established its beachhead the next day against fanatical Japanese resistance, and by afternoon, U.S. tanks were rolling in toward the island's interior.

Back at Dobodura, standing in line for mess that night, a few of us fell to talking of the foot soldiers who had to hit the beaches of these rain-soaked islands in the midst of that unremitting downpour, with mortar and machine-gun nests aimed at them from the trees.

"If you were one of those guys," asked a copilot from the 529th, "what would you be wanting for Christmas?"

"I dunno," I said, reaching for a note of levity, "maybe an umbrella?"

"No, no! That's us," he replied. "*We're* their umbrella, the only one they're gonna get!"

Then he said, "Tell you what I'd want. I'd want to wake up and learn I'd just been dreamin' it."

"Sure," I agreed. "That'd be nice." But I kept thinking, *We were their umbrellas*, the only protection some of those guys would get.

From that time, right up through Christmas Eve, we flew almost daily raids over Cape Gloucester and Cape Hoskins. Alongside 43rd and 90th Bomb Group crews, we placed so many big bombs on the

Japanese airfields to the north of that island, that we couldn't imagine any runways or support facilities left intact. Weather had improved, and we were putting 1,000-pound bombs right on target. Col. Miller, who flew personally in as many raids as any of the rest of us, estimated that we of the strike force were pulverizing those targets with an average daily devastation of 260 tons of bombs.

Bill Miller that month was awarded his eagles, the rank of full colonel. The crews, on learning this at one of our daily premission briefings, applauded our new "bird colonel" lustily. Not one of us doubted for a second that he'd earned the promotion. Miller, for his part, expressed regret to us all that we were spending the Christmas holidays there on New Guinea, with no celebration. He personally promised us a big Christmas dinner with all the trimmings when we finished our job there and got back to Fenton. I realized that it was December 22, my twenty-first birthday.

# 24

STRESS, RELIEF, AND THE SWEET SORROW

THE HECTIC EMERGENCY PACE was beginning to take its toll on aircraft maintenance. The local ground crews were surely doing their best to keep us flying, but the abbreviated time between missions allowed the two mechanics assigned to each B-24 inadequate opportunity to check and test all parts, as our regular crews back at Fenton had done with such painstaking care. Several of our Liberators were developing mechanical failures and having to be sidelined for repairs.

Planes were not the only things getting stressed out. Twice we were awakened at two o'clock in the morning for predawn takeoffs in two hours. The pace, the weather, the tension over target, and the constant formation flying were causing a certain amount of wear and tear on our nervous systems. Not to mention the soggy clothes, the ubiquitous mosquitoes, and the lack of sleep, which combined to produce a shortness of temper. Some of us, for the first time, were getting irritable with one another.

Early one morning I staggered into the chow line, trying to force sleep out of my brain and concentrate on what we'd been told at the briefing. I'd just taken a spoonful of unappealing powdered eggs and filled my cup with hot coffee, when I was blindsided by the force of a human body stumbling into the back of my left shoulder. The sudden force caused me to lose my grip on the cup. The hot liquid splashed out in a torrent, all over my combat fatigues.

Whirling in unconscious reflex and emitting an involuntary oath, I'd called the fellow a "careless son of a bitch!" before I realized that he'd fallen onto the floor of the mess hall. I know I didn't hit him, and I didn't think I'd shoved him, but my utensils had clattered to the floor, and it must have looked as though I'd knocked him down in a fit of rage. Suddenly everybody in the mess hall was looking at me.

Then I recognized the man, and felt ashamed. I self-consciously offered him a hand, too embarrassed and unnerved by the situation to know what to say. It was a poor old boy who'd been pointed out to me a day or so earlier. He'd taken to wandering in and out of the early morning mess hall lineups, sometimes drunk, before a mission takeoff. His story, as I'd heard it, was a sad one.

The man was no longer on active flying status. Nobody seemed to know what his current assignment was. He had been a member of a crew—a waist gunner, I think—and had flown a goodly number of missions. One day he was ill—some said "hung over," though I never had the straight of that—and for whatever reason unable to fly. His pilot had to fill in with a substitute from another crew. The plane was shot down that day, all the crew killed in action. This poor guy went into a terrible funk, blaming himself. According to the story, he fantasized a scenario in which it was all his fault that his buddies were dead. Perhaps he imagined he'd have been able to down their attacker before the crippling cannon shot, had he been aboard.

There is, I have since read, a recognized mental syndrome called survivor's guilt. Maybe that's what my friend, Joe Vick, had felt. But Joe snapped out of it, or seemed to. What happens to fellows who crack up under the strain of extreme or prolonged exposure to combat catastrophes has many names. In World War I they called it "shell shock." In our war, the prevalent Army Air Corps term was "combat fatigue." A new refinement in our understanding of war's lingering effects came following the Vietnam conflict. It's called post-traumatic stress disorder. All this, I believe, is valid, and none of us is immune. We should thank God if we've escaped the snare, though I may have been skating near its claws that day.

DECEMBER 26 WAS A DAY to remember for many of us in the 380th. Shaken out of our sleep at 2 A.M., aircrews were readied for predawn takeoffs two hours later. Col. Miller and a select crew in the lead aircraft, *Gypsy*, lifted off the runway into the darkness, followed by all the 380th crews with operative aircraft on Dobodura. Fifty-six other Liberator crews from other units followed in a succession of takeoffs that included ninety medium bombers as well.

There may have been 170 aircraft in all, ready to rendezvous and form up on *Gypsy* over Sakar Island, between New Guinea and the New Britain coast. Our aim was to drop a crushing load of explosive power on Japanese defenses at Cape Gloucester. Each B-24 carried eight 1,000-pound bombs.

It was invasion day. The fabled leathernecks of the U.S. 1st Marine Division were piling off ship decks into landing craft for their assault on New Britain's northwest land mass.

There was a lot of initial confusion as all these planes converged in the limited space above Sakar Island, some arriving on different headings. Our nerves grew as taut as banjo strings while pilots edged and maneuvered to avoid colliding in the faintly growing light.

Lieutenant Harold Mulhollen, newly promoted to an aircraft commander and a buddy of our missing Bob Russell, suddenly saw another B-24 heading directly toward him in the half-darkness from his immediate right. He quickly did the only thing he could do to avoid being rammed. He instinctively threw his B-24 into a left-spinning dive. From our perch at about 10,000 feet, Mulhollen's craft plunged almost straight down in a vertical cycle, spinning to the left. The plane began to plummet. Down it went, for a thousand, two thousand, three thousand feet, more than a mile down, nose first.

Harold and his copilot, Russ Fleming, in a remarkable feat of mental concentration, sat there, steadily applying opposite controls with all their strength until finally, to the vast relief of those watching from above, the plane pulled out at what, from our altitude, looked like a perilously low level above the sea. It later was reported to be a little over 3,000 feet when the nose finally pulled up level. Those who watched nervously from our higher altitude thought of the performance of these two levelheaded pilots as little short of miraculous. That plane, loaded with eight 1,000-pounders, may have been the only B-24 ever to survive the stress of a vertical spinning dive of that duration. Mulhollen headed the stressed-out craft back to a safe landing at Dobodura, its fuselage torqued just slightly out of shape.

When Mulhollen and Fleming pulled their disfigured B-24 into a revetment and walked away, the story goes, someone asked Harold and Russ what thoughts ran through their minds as they tried to pull the plane out of its spinning dive. Mulhollen is supposed to have quipped, "Well, we were thinking of how much that airplane had cost, of course. After all, my father's a taxpayer."

Mulhollen's skills were celebrated heartily in our squadron, but far too briefly. In one of war's sad ironies, he and his crew were shot down over northern New Guinea about ten days later.

THE BOMB LOAD our airborne armada placed on Gloucester's target hill that morning was awesome. We didn't drop our bombs by individual sightings, as we bombardiers had been accustomed to doing, but "toggled" them with a little hand switch, off the lead plane's sighting. As soon as he saw the first bomb leave the leader's plane, each bombardier in each close cluster released his plane's bombs. They fell literally like great buckets of rain.

Lying in wait offshore were the ships and landing craft filled with marines and armored landing vehicles. We discovered later that day that the pulverizing strikes we'd rained down upon the site had been so devastating that they'd driven Japanese defense forces into the hills in disarray. The first wave of the marine landings went so smoothly that our leatherneck troops suffered no casualties in establishing their broad and advancing beachhead. That was a good feeling.

But the fight wasn't over. That afternoon, a large battery of more than sixty Zekes and about twenty-five Japanese bombers based at Rabaul assaulted the second wave of marines as it approached the beach. Japanese bombers sank one of our destroyers and damaged two others before being driven off by navy and Air Corps fighter planes. Still, the marines were ashore, and moving steadily inland.

WITH U.S. GROUND FORCES making progress on New Britain, General MacArthur's command began to focus on trying to wrest the northern and western two-thirds of New Guinea from Japan's clutches. This would be a more daunting task due to the vastness and density of the huge island and our foes' deeply dug-in positions.

New Guinea is considered by many to be the world's largest island. Shaped somewhat like the silhouette of a wild turkey roosting on a limb, it lies above northeastern Australia, with its northwestern-most point reaching halfway from Australia's northern coast to the Philippines. A high central plateau runs, east–west, from the tip of the turkey's tail to the beak, almost 1,600 miles, with rugged peaks that rise above 15,000 feet. The jungle is dense and physically forbidding, peopled by different native tribes, some of them in those days practitioners of cannibalism.

The last two missions for our crew came just at year's end. We bombed the well-defended coastal airdrome at Alexishafen and the Allied landing site at Saidor. Ours was the lead plane that morning. My turn to aim the bombs, while others toggled theirs off my lead. In my hands was a recent photograph of the area. I'd carefully color-coded the linear brush-covered segment from which Japanese gunners manned a defensive line of artillery behind entrenched machine-gun nests.

Offshore, we could see our ships, and the first line of landing craft already moving shoreward as we began our bomb run. It was a

# THE FLYING CIRCUS

proud sight. The morning was breaking clear. The landmarks below were plainly visible, our precise target area unmistakably identifiable.

I MUSN'T THINK of the people down there, I had taught myself, amid the convoluting vines and glaucous foliage underneath that line of palms—but focus instead on the iron and cruel steel contorted into cannon and machine guns, ready now to burst forth with their frenzied chatter, ripping fire into our marines and infantrymen. It was a mental game I played. And now, by deliberate transference, I concentrated only on that piece of ground. The hands on the bombsight became extensions of my mind. Focus, now. I lined up the crosshairs on the chosen spot for the first of our string of bombs, and held it there. Held it there. Right there, ahead and below, right *there* (where enemy gunners were nervously turning their own gun-sights, ready to lay down a wall of fire intended to decimate our landing party). *Focus.* Steady focus on the spot.

"Bombs away!" I didn't stop to think this was the last time I'd hear that phrase aboard *Gus's Bus.* An explosive eruption of dirt and debris and a puffy cloud, right there! The spot! The right spot! Then the other bombs, cratering in train, directly along the center of our targeted line. Quickly now, a string of great chunks of churned earth kicking up on either side, as 1,000-pounders from our wingmen and the on-following formation chewed up the ground in a massive upheaval, along and across the whole area of Japanese firepower.

There came a sense of relief, almost instantaneous. I do not even remember, strangely, whether we encountered balls of anti-aircraft fire or if enemy interceptors came up to meet us. I don't recall anything about our flight back, or the debriefing at Dobodura later that morning. My mind still re-creates, however—all these years later—the sight of our troop ships to seaward and our yellow-colored landing craft approaching shore.

That afternoon, somebody from Operations sent word to our crew, and presumably the others who participated, that the landing had been secured without a single U.S. casualty. That was the best

188

feeling of all. Well, almost the best. Soon, that fluffy cushion of self-congratulation was subsumed in even more euphoric news. Word came from Bratton that our crew was free to return, as soon as we could pack and get takeoff clearance, to our base at Fenton.

Free! Our work was done. We'd performed thirty combat missions and chalked up more than three hundred hours of combat flying time. It was a relief and a letdown, all at the same time. One thing was sure: none of us would miss Dobodura.

BACK AT FENTON, the next days passed in a haze. Our crews, so long absent in New Guinea, now had our delayed Christmas dinner with all available trimmings. We discovered that, in our absence, a troupe of Hollywood actors headed by Gary Cooper had visited Fenton strip and entertained the main party that remained there. We had also missed an even more auspicious visit by General George C. Marshall, the general's general to whom Eisenhower and Patton and MacArthur all reported. Our little tent city was on the map, and our 380th Flying Circus had become a recognized entity by those in high places!

But with it all, there set in an ineradicable note of sadness. At least half the original aircrew party had been shot down, and now the rest of us were completing our tours, one by one replaced and reassigned.

Languidly I recalled the nights and afternoons when we'd played poker at the club, and I—conscious of my married status and thinking of our future, and of Mab's letters telling me how many war bonds she'd put aside for us each month from my pay allotment—had confined myself to games with penny-ante stakes. What a funny irony, I reflected now—risking my life each mission we'd flown but too tight to risk a few bucks. I remembered now the nights we'd sung our own parodies to "Bless 'Em All," the British army song favored by our Aussie hosts. In the last stanza we'd extemporized the woeful line, "We won't see the Golden Shore/ In nineteen forty-four / Cheer up, my lads, bless them all."

So, 'forty-four was here, and some of us *would* see the Golden Gate again, after all. Those of us who'd been lucky. Somehow, through these months, I had never really doubted that I'd make it back. The certainty I felt, admittedly, defied logic. I vaguely wondered a time or two if some like Dave Lippencott or John Farrington or Rocky Stoner, now all presumed dead, had been as confident as I. And as the months and weeks went by, odds lengthening realistically with each safe completion of another mission, I knew that my faith was occasionally inclined to falter. By some unfathomable grace of God, we'd made it.

Gus alone among us opted to extend his tour, newly appointed as group operations officer and promoted to major. Awaiting our orders alongside men from our other dismantling Circus crews, the rest of us watched as one after another of those with whom we'd come to Australia the previous April was flown to Townsville and then Brisbane for passage home aboard a Liberty Ship. As if to add finality to what had been our crew, like a period at the end of a sentence, our old plane, *Gus's Bus*, was assigned to a replacement crew and cracked up beyond repair within two weeks on the Dobodura runway.

At Townsville, General George Kenney pinned the Distinguished Flying Cross and a couple of other medals on my tunic, and on March 1, an assorted number of us left Brisbane Harbor bound for San Francisco. Aussie crowds came out to bid us farewell, and seventeen days later—on St. Patrick's Day—we steamed beneath the Golden Gate Bridge and disembarked to the accompaniment of a live military marching band and the cheers of an American crowd. However commonplace our individual service might have been, people treated us all like heroes.

A generation later, I would remember the heady joys of this day, and wish painfully for Mab's and my son, and military contemporaries of his returning from assignments in Vietnam, that they could have savored such a royal welcome of their own.

Within short days of that dockside welcome, my train arrived in the early dawn at the depot in Weatherford, Texas. There, in the faint light, I saw my bride, my father and mother, my sisters, and Reverend Ray Ohman, the minister of our church, standing beside the platform. Martha Thomas, who had cooked for our family since the day we moved into that big old house on Oak and Waco streets, had prepared a country breakfast of fried chicken, biscuits, rice and gravy. The pungency of the chicken and the heady, doughy vapors rising from a hot, newly opened biscuit, filled my nostrils, and my mouth watered. I knew I was home.

The war wasn't over, of course. There'd be other assignments after that wondrous six weeks' leave, three at home and three more of "recreation leave" at Miami Beach for Mab and me. Under new orders, I trained and indoctrinated aircrews en route to overseas assignments. They were routed through Lincoln Army Air Base in Nebraska, where some of us—who'd recently been through what lay ahead for them—tried to give them every preparation we could.

After the war, we picked up the threads of our interrupted friendships. Gus and Bob Russell both flew for Eastern Airlines until Gus took an administrative post with the Federal Aviation Administration from which he retired in due course. Bob finally found his niche as an artist. Pat became both a CPA and a lawyer.

Jack Bratton became a general, continuing to serve in the Air Force in command positions of increasing national importance, including inspector general of the 2nd Air Force and Commander of U-2 Operations. Red Weinstein rounded out a successful career as a banker in Philadelphia.

The base adjutant at Williams Field when we were there, Major John Rhodes, was elected to Congress from Arizona and chosen Minority Leader of the U.S. House of Representatives. Virgil Stevens's home in Fort Worth was a routine overnight hospitality station on the itinerary of almost every visiting Aussie who had served with the 380th.

I was at Gus's funeral in 1989, and still carry in my pocket a laminated Prayer of St. Francis, a souvenir of Pat's funeral mass in 1994. Tally Koumarelos and I visited a few months before his death in 1999. There are days when I feel we're still flying together.

But that is the musing of an old man, which is what I am now. Let's think instead of that cornucopia of good things, of gifts and dreams and broad attitudinal changes that our common victory over the Axis powers in World War II wrought upon our land and world, to the enrichment of us all. Without an appreciation of that bountiful legacy, our tale is not complete. The spirit and energy of our heterogeneous mass of returning war veterans permeated and influenced major changes in America's lifestyle. That's what I'd like to explore with you now, in the Afterword.

## AFTERWORD

THE TRAIN FROM San Antonio made a joyous *clickity-clack* as its wheels rolled along the steel rails toward Fort Worth. The rhythm congealed into a quicker tempo, and then a steady hum as the train picked up speed and more miles disappeared behind us. It was very early that May morning in 1945, still pitch-dark outside. But most of the auxiliary reading lights were still on in our coach car. Most of the northbound passengers were too keyed up with excitement to sleep. The din of a dozen or more private conversations converged into a single blurry buzz, interrupted now and then by a sudden burst of laughter.

The fellow sitting in the aisle seat beside mine had finally dozed off. I sat silently with my thoughts, feeling a mellow glow and waiting for the dawn. I'd be back home in Weatherford before noon, dressed in my newly purchased civvies. The suit, bought at Joske's, had cost twenty-seven dollars. For most of the passengers in the car, the northbound train was heading toward home.

Twenty-five or thirty of us, released from active duty that day at Fort Sam Houston's mustering-out center, carried our honorable discharge certificates as though they were passports to heaven. Each had served in some branch of the army for most or all of the past three and a half years. We were among the first released on the army's new "point system." The worldwide military menace had narrowed to the largely defeated but stubborn, resistant remnant of tattered imperial power in Japan. The end finally in sight, our government began the process of mustering out those who'd served longest, been most exposed to combat, been awarded the greatest number of military decorations, or some combination of the above.

I'd been offered my choice between this early mustering out or an appointment to Fort Leavenworth's Command and General Staff School, with promise of promotion should I choose to stay in the peacetime army. That choice was easy. I had never desired a military career. As one of my fellow retirees had said that afternoon, "The only thing I've ever really wanted from the army was *out*." Actually, I reflected, the army had treated me well enough. I just had other things in mind.

God, was I glad to be back! Eager to get started on a career. While in Lincoln I had lined up a job that I looked forward to performing in Texas. I'd be traveling, selling memberships and recruiting other sales representatives in the then fledgling National Federation of Small Business. Its headquarters were in San Mateo, California. I was anxious to start making some money.

On January 31, just about ten months after my return from overseas, our first child arrived. James III, now four months old, would need a lot of things. I'd rented a small, two-bedroom house with one bath, and had committed to looking at a 1937 Dodge owned and driven by an elderly Weatherford couple. Until I located one in good shape that wouldn't make too big a dent in our modest savings, I could perform my business-related travel by bus or train.

The guys I knew who shared my position of civilian reentry didn't expect too much too soon in the way of breaks. We were all willing to work, and determined to carve out a living. The universality of service didn't mean we all had the same expectations.

About the only two really big hopes, or anything approaching consensus on any right or entitlement for having fought for our country, could be summed up in two phrases: *jobs enough* to go around, and *no more war*.

● ● ●

OUR NATIONAL military victory was not the exclusive property of we who had seen combat, or who had worn a uniform. Almost every citizen had endured genuine sacrifice and made very real contributions to the collective effort. Never before nor since, in my opinion, has this country experienced such enthusiastic unity of purpose.

Those who returned from the war, however, brought with us a number of hard-won lessons. One was *inclusiveness*. Almost all of us had absorbed something very valuable from the continuous mixing, working and cooperating with people of other religious affiliations, of other economic strata, and from other regions of our land. We had worked with these others to win the war. Maybe we could work together to secure the fruits of peace?

What we'd gained was a far better understanding of, and harmony of purpose with, the wider spectrum of our fellow Americans. We'd had to cast aside the restraining remnants of local chauvinisms, ethnic schisms, religious bigotry, and regional mistrusts. In the words of our pledge of allegiance, we'd been becoming more nearly "*one* nation, *indivisible*."

We remained, of course, free individuals. There was no uniformity of opinion or conformity of creed among us. It was just that, instead of resenting our diversity—or merely tolerating it—we were learning to celebrate it.

For some of our contemporaries, the widening horizons of inclusion had not yet stretched to offer economic equality to women or social and political equality to African-Americans, but seeds of acceptance had been widely sowed, and in time they'd bear fruit.

Before the 1940s expired, U.S. military units previously separated by race would be integrated. In four more years, the U.S. Supreme Court would outlaw racial segregation of public schools. It was, in large part, our wartime experience with women's auxiliary military services (WAAFs, WACs, and WAVEs) and with "Rosie the Riveter" war workers that began rapidly opening careers and professions of all kinds to women.

Another important change, I think, was the *growth of confidence* in our own abilities, individually and collectively. Our personal and social ambitions grew. We dared to believe in the reality of upward mobility—and not just for ourselves, but for the American rank and file. Our rising tide would lift many other ships along with our own.

As a result of these two forces working in tandem, a dynamic developed that exceeded even our own fondest expectations. Never had any country enjoyed such a mutually reinforcing agenda of enlightening, enriching, and democratizing expansion of opportunities and socially uplifting reforms as the United States experienced in the twenty years that followed World War II.

These phenomena were not the exclusive work of either political party. For eight of those productive years, the White House and Capitol Hill were in the hands of rival political parties. But rivals then, in that climate, were more friendly, more courteous, more mutually respectful than they would later become.

Much of what happened in those years was achieved by private individuals, armed now with more education, more optimism, more faith in the attainability of their own ambitions. To the extent this progress was inspired by political leaders, we must bear in mind that the great spurts of growth launched by public policy decisions could never have been so spectacularly successful but for the wholehearted response they received from the millions of returning servicemen and -women who helped make the public dreams become realities.

The GI Joes and Janes were not timid. Their wartime achievements had taught them firsthand that great goals could be attained through their united effort. Bold challenges did not discourage them, nor mediocre achievements satisfy them. Here are a few of our generation's dramatic landmark initiatives:

### THE GI BILL

QUITE PROBABLY the best investment of tax dollars this nation ever made—the one that paid the richest dividends to our country—was the Servicemen's Readjustment Act of 1944, more popularly known as the GI Bill of Rights.

The bill passed by Congress and signed by President Roosevelt on June 2, 1944, was a triumph of those in and out of Congress who thought big. Originally launched as a proposal of the American Legion, an organization founded by World War I veterans, the bill undertook an astounding array of practical, down-to-earth benefits for the new generation of returning vets.

Two things that caught our attention when we first heard of the program in Australia were what sounded like extraordinarily generous opportunities—to attend college at government expense, and to borrow through government-insured, low-interest loans to build and own homes for the families we looked forward to having. For many, perhaps most of the GIs, these benefits seemed almost too good to be true.

Actually, there was more to the program. The same sort of publicly backed loans would be available to veterans who wanted to start a business of their own, or buy an interest in an existing one. And for those cut loose without an awaiting job or any idea of where to find one, there'd be a one-year grace period in which they wouldn't have to starve while trying to locate work. Back home in Weatherford, this came to be known as the 52/20 Club. For up to one full year, jobless veterans could draw $20 a week (a gift, not a loan) to tide them over while they sought employment.

In Congress, the GI Bill's sponsors fought off various attacks from others who wanted to cut it back, shrink or curtail it for fear of its possible ultimate cost. But—backed by World War I veterans who remembered postwar periods of joblessness and tough times—it appealed mightily to a nation full of folks who'd suffered during the Depression and now saw a chance to help their war-absent family members start anew. The legislators who wanted to do more triumphed handily over the hesitant ones who would do less.

The GI Bill was no miserly gesture.

◉ ◉ ◉

A STUPENDOUS RESPONSE from the returning veteran population greeted the menu of educational opportunities offered. Thousands of additional classrooms had to be built to accommodate the influx of vets! Before the war, in my contemporary crowd of college-age youth, fewer than 5 percent were finishing four years of college. Lack of money had been the primary impediment for most.

In 1940, for example, only 109,000 men and 77,000 women graduated with bachelor degrees. By 1949, thanks to the stimulus of the GI Bill, the annual graduation rate had soared to 528,000 men and 103,000 women. More than a fourfold increase overall, and among American men almost *five times as many* were graduating from American colleges and universities with the academic credentials for good-paying jobs! Others availed themselves of a trade school eduction, or practical vocational and apprenticeship training.

There sprang up an entirely new outlook toward advanced learning. Total enrollment in our institutions of higher education among nonveterans was also zooming. No longer was a college education considered a luxury to which only an elite minority might aspire. The numbers were astounding! In 1939, the total college enrollment in America was about 1.5 million. By 1949, it was 2.6 million. And our vets' generation was fighting to see to it that their children would also be upwardly mobile. By 1969, when three of my offspring were in college, enrollment was up to eight million.

And here is the surprising thing: The educational boom which the GI Bill set in motion not only enriched the country in educational attainment and productive scientific inquiry, resulting in expanded buying power, medical leaps forward, and a richer social fabric; it also paid off in cold cash for the U.S. Treasury itself! The government's tuition expenditures and collateral benefits did not add to the national debt. Far from it! As the beneficiaries qualified for far better wages and higher family incomes, they paid billions more in taxes throughout their working careers. Studies estimated that, by the end of the 1960s, every dollar spent on the variegated benefits of the GI Bill had repaid the Treasury approximately eight times over.

In all, some 2.2 million veterans benefited directly from the educational opportunities offered in the GI Bill. This comes to about a third of all who served.

Add to these the many thousands more who swelled the ranks of home ownership, expanding local city and county coffers with their property taxes. New homes for veterans fueled the development of a relatively new social phenomenon, the American suburb. Before the war, fewer than a third of our nation's families owned any equity in the houses they occupied. Two-thirds were renters. Due to the stimulus of guaranteed low-interest loans, those figures, by the mid-1960s, had reversed themselves. Now, two out of three families were homeowners.

In the process of all this, America was doing much more than just helping veterans. We were creating a new national reality—a much bigger, wider, and more pervasive middle class. Another, even more egalitarian perspective might be that we were actually moving toward that even more elusive goal—a classless society.

We had worried that there'd not be enough jobs to absorb the huge influx of some six million military veterans suddenly flooding the civilian economy, looking for work. That was the silent bugaboo that lingered in the minds of many of my contemporaries. Former vice president Henry A. Wallace began a campaign calling for action to provide 60 million jobs. Many people thought that demand illusory, wildly excessive, far too visionary and impossible to attain.

When Wallace ran for president in 1948, heading a third party "Progressive" ticket, his slate brought up the distant rear while President Harry Truman surprisingly trounced Thomas E. Dewey to gain reelection. Guess what? Wallace's dream came true. American payrolls were employing 60 million bread winners by 1960, and 80 million by the end of the '60s.

### BIPARTISAN POLICY

THE TOGETHERNESS IDEAL percolated up to the top rungs of our government. Neither Democrats nor Republicans wanted another bitter partisan bloodletting like the one that followed World

War I. Then a little "coterie of willful men" (President Woodrow Wilson's words) in the U.S. Senate had cheerfully scuttled Wilson's grand dream of U.S. participation in the League of Nations. Led by Senator Henry Cabot Lodge, Republican of Massachusetts, the opposition denied sufficient votes to ratify the Treaty of Versailles.

Wilson had barnstormed the country pleading his cause, worked and worried himself into a crippling stroke from which he never fully recovered. Many believe that this vituperative feud laid the groundwork for our country's long dalliance with isolationism, thus making World War II unavoidable.

Now, at war's end, isolationism was dead. Wendell Willkie, the 1940 Republican standard-bearer, wrote his well-received book, *One World*, making a strong case for an international outlook. Leaders in both major political parties embraced the basic, new concept of a bipartisan foreign policy.

When President Harry Truman approached Republican senator Arthur Vandenberg of Michigan, then chairman of the Senate Committee on Foreign Relations, and asked for his party's legislative cooperation, Vandenberg promised it, with only one caveat: If you expect us to be with you on the landing, you have to bring us with you at the takeoff. Cooperation was a two-way street. And its chances flourished with advance consultation, both sides learned.

Well-known World War II military leaders were sometimes at the forefront of major groundbreaking policy movements. General George C. Marshall, Truman's appointee as Secretary of State, reversed the stagnant rules of disengagement (To the victor belong the spoils!). Instead of gouging the shattered remnants of Germany, Italy, and Japan for monetary reparations, the War Department shipped 1.2 million tons of foodstuffs, mostly grains, to feed hungry German people threatened with starvation in the summer of 1947.

The much broader Marshall Plan of that same year earmarked substantial amounts of money to help the fallen foes get back onto their feet, while also assisting our former allies in the rehabilitation of Western Europe. General Douglas MacArthur, meanwhile, was guiding the peaceful renewal of Japan in the form of an elective democratic society. Winston Churchill called the Marshall Plan the "most unsordid" act in history.

In the newborn spirit of cooperation on foreign affairs that pervaded the American political establishment, a Republican congressman, Representative Christian Herter, took a lead role in helping Democratic President Truman pass the Marshall Plan's enabling legislation. In sharp contrast to the venomous post-World War I squabbles, the bipartisan alliance, particularly on matters of foreign policy, held firm through the 1950s and for a time beyond.

### INTERSTATE HIGHWAYS

ONE OF THE BOLDEST domestic ventures of the postwar period was President Dwight D. Eisenhower's Interstate Highway System, which I had the heady privilege of being somewhat helpful in developing. When the president first advanced that grand design in 1955, Americans were trying to cram some 63 million vehicles onto a road structure designed for about half that number.

My personal fortunes, afloat on the tide of good luck, a lot of work, and our rising national economy, had made it possible for me to enjoy direct participation in this national adventure. Returning to Weatherford at war's end, we'd rented a small house while getting on our feet financially. For almost two years, I enjoyed my role with the Small Business federation. Incomewise, we were doing fairly well. The war, however, had not been kind to my father's business, which was devoted to helping retail merchants develop and expand their trade territories. It needed an inoculation of new capital to resuscitate itself, and to recruit and train a new sales force to replace the one drawn away into essential wartime activity.

I borrowed from our local bank on a 4 percent GI Loan and purchased from Dad a one-fourth interest in his firm. The timing was perfect, and with a burst of fresh effort, we had the business flourishing in a short time. In 1949, at age twenty-six, I was drafted by a committee of local citizens to run for mayor of Weatherford.

Elected, I spent every morning in the family business, turning my attentions in the afternoons to City Hall. Doing justice to both out of the same twenty-four-hour day was a challenge I enjoyed. The adrenaline it invoked became, my family would joke, addictive.

We welcomed our second child and first daughter, Ginger, in 1949, and built a three-bedroom house that cost what I then considered the extortionate sum of $20,000. In 1954, I ran for and won election to the U.S. Congress. There I was appointed to the Public Works Committee, where I soon found myself heavily involved with President Eisenhower's highway proposal.

Highway building, like other primarily civilian needs, had been discontinued during the war so that we could devote the money and manpower to military priorities. Even basic maintenance of the civilian infrastructure had been relegated to the back burner. No new cars were made from 1941 to 1945; older cars, nursed and coaxed through the war, were now wearing out.

At first, the pent-up demand for automobiles forced dealers in 1945 and '46 to place eager new car customers on waiting lists, as reactivated assembly lines began rolling off the first new models since Pearl Harbor. No other symbol of America's postwar affluence—not even that wondrous new living room marvel, the TV set—rivaled the purchase of private autos. The automobile industry by the 1950s was our nation's biggest employer.

Until this time, highway building and upkeep had been essentially a state effort. There was little uniformity in design. Drivers would know the moment they crossed a state line by the often-sudden change in road design, width, and quality of maintenance.

In trying to move large, heavy-duty military items like missiles and tanks cross-country by road from manufacturing plants to shipping docks, Eisenhower had seen many of the random nonsystem's glaring inadequacies: low bridges, narrow roads and culverts, poor paving, and twists and turns that made our task of moving military shipments slower, more dangerous, and more difficult.

But the president's vision was broader than sheer military necessity. It dealt with things increasingly precious to our more and more mobile people. Highway safety was objective number one. Already, highway fatalities accounted for more deaths among Americans aged eighteen through twenty-five than any other cause. And among all Americans, traffic accidents killed more people each year than anything else except heart attacks and strokes.

Still, since Winston Churchill's 1947 Fulton, Missouri, speech warning of an *Iron Curtain*, we had been increasingly drawn into that titanic competition of fear, propaganda, science, and ideas known as the Cold War. The United States and the Soviet Union, each fearing and neither understanding the other, became locked in rival efforts, each determined to win the peoples of the underdeveloped world to its side. Commentators dubbed it a war for the minds of men. It was comforting to supporters of the highway program to have also a potential military reason to support the roads we knew the country needed. So, Congress shamelessly gained public support by officially naming the project the Interstate and *National Defense* Highway System.

Eisenhower's plan was ambitious and sweeping. He would build a nationwide network—41,000 miles—of multilaned, modern, safe, and efficient superhighways to tie our nation together. These ribbons of concrete and steel would span rivers, deserts, and mountains to connect up every American city of 100,000 people or more. It would move people and goods safely and swiftly.

It is no exaggeration to say that this was the most extensive, and expensive, public-works undertaking in human history. In size and scope it dwarfed the pyramids, the Roman aqueducts, the Great Wall of China.

How to pay for it? Well, General Lucius Clay, who'd been Ike's point man on the project, didn't exactly know. His suggestion: Just sell long-term government bonds (30- or 40-year payouts) and decide where to get the money as the bonds came due. But several of us on the House Public Works Committee thought this was dodging the issue, making the roads cost more and adding unacceptably to the nation's long-term debt. Through Speaker Sam Rayburn's intercession, our group got an appointment with Eisenhower.

Pledging support for the road program, the spokesman for the group, a Democrat from Minnesota named John Blatnik, said the committee would prefer to pay as we go. Borrow nothing, we suggested. Create a Highway Trust Fund, financed by road-user taxes—a few cents on a gallon of gas, a small tax on truck tires, since heavier trucks wear out the roads faster—and use that trust fund only for roads. Build only as fast as the money comes in, no faster. "This way," we said to the president, "we'll not be calling on our children to pay for roads we've been wearing out; we'll be giving them a gift of usable, paid-for roads, not a pile of debt." Wrinkling his brow, the president thought for a minute, then said he liked it. "If you think you can sell that to the American people, good luck! You have my blessing."

And that is exactly what we did.

Here again, a victory for action and growth. And faith in the people. Fears that there'd be loud public outcries over the taxes to pay for the roads were unfounded. They sold the American public short. People were glad to get the roads. They knew they'd have to be paid for, and they didn't want to encumber their offspring with debt.

This highway system generated a veritable deluge of private investments along these routes. New hotels, restaurants, automotive service stations. Every public dollar spent on interstate roads set into motion at least nine dollars of private investments in new job-creating enterprises. New payrolls mushroomed, and Treasury balances were assuaged by their additional tax inflow. The Trust Fund, from the plan's earliest days, was paying off like an overly generous slot machine. And our national economy slipped into a still higher gear.

The trust fund concept even became a model for the building and upgrading of much-needed airports in our ever more mobile society. The jet-set age is taking off and landing on pay-as-we-go runways from terminals erected from a pay-as-we-go Airport and Airway Development Trust Fund.

## THE SPACE AGE

SLIGHTLY DIFFERENT CONSIDERATIONS motivated our great leap forward into space. Here, the Cold War's uneasy balance vis-à-vis the Soviet Union in military readiness and scientific supremacy moved us into our all-out effort to catch and surpass our international rival.

In the autumn of 1957, the Soviet Union successfully launched *Sputnik I*, the world's first artificial satellite, marking the start of the U.S.–USSR space race. On April 12, 1961, Russian Cosmonaut Yuri Gagarin became the first man in space, flying alone in a Soviet spacecraft named *Vostok I*. America was profoundly shocked, shamed, and challenged.

Our rivals for world leadership had the jump on us. Most Americans had no real conception of space science, of what this all meant. We just knew it was frightening and something had to be done.

Among private citizens, the development conveyed a widespread impression of pending doom. More than one constituent expressed the prevalent fear by asking, "Does this mean the Communists can fly a bunch of spaceships up there somewhere that we can't reach with our missiles, and just say 'Drop your guns; we've gotcha covered'?"

We were behind, no doubt about it. With the help of some smart East German scientists, Russian leaders had been working silently on space research for several years and now had taken a commanding lead in what became a feverish competition.

It was not until 1958 that our National Aeronautics and Space Administration (NASA) was formally launched. By 1960, there were 10,000 people working at the space agency. This number would grow to 36,000 by 1966.

It was President John F. Kennedy's dramatic promise in a nationally televised speech to Congress on May 25, 1961, that captured the public imagination and riveted the American nation into the concerted, high-priority drive that our space effort became.

With vivid clarity I can remember our instant reaction to Kennedy's bold, unequivocating pledge to land a man on the moon and bring him safely back to Earth "before this decade is out." That unleashed, in Congress and throughout the nation, a continuous outpouring of ungrudging public support.

This pledge was so audacious that Democratic and Republican lawmakers, uncertain just what arcane methodologies and expenditures it might require, were united in the determination to give to the effort whatever priority and financial backing was needed.

The cost of the Apollo project would eventually total $24 billion. The *New York Times* space editor, John Noble Wilford, called it the "greatest mobilization of men and resources ever undertaken for a peaceful project of science and exploration."

So much for Christopher Columbus and Queen Isabella.

NASA's actual launching operations were performed at Cape Canaveral, Florida, and the Manned Spacecraft Center in Houston. As an outgrowth of this venture, there has grown up a far-flung network of private manufacturers and suppliers of scientific studies, as well as highly specialized equipment.

Early on, Dr. Wernher Von Braun was assembling an impressive team of engineers, including the German scientists who'd developed the German V-2, the world's first successful launch rocket. While the actual spacecraft were assembled and built in a specially constructed thirty-six-story building at Cape Canaveral, the rockets that powered the spacecraft were put together under Von Braun's direction at the army's Redstone Arsenal.

Twenty days before President Kennedy's 1961 speech, Alan Shepard lifted his space capsule into the realm of space for fifteen minutes, becoming the first American human to fly in space. Eight months later, John Glenn became the first to orbit the earth.

After as many as twenty more heavily monitored flights by NASA's skilled and celebrity-status astronauts, on a six-day mission in July of 1969—within the time frame promised by President Kennedy—Neil

Armstrong, Michael Collins, and Edwin (Buzz) Aldrin reached the moon. As Collins kept the spacecraft operative, Armstrong and Aldrin landed, took rock samples, and planted an American flag before returning.

By then, we had captured the lead in space exploration from our Cold War competition. And, in time, both nations recognized the mutual advantages of joint cooperation—rather than competition—in space exploration.

IT IS HARD TO MEASURE the extent to which our individual lifestyles have been affected by the national space program. Literally thousands of scientific and engineering "spinoffs" have entered the field of medical practice, auto and aircraft engineering, computer technology, nutrition improvements, and environmental science based on space discoveries.

Because of these improvements, humans today benefit from greatly improved systems for such assorted things as detecting breast cancer, faster computer processing, enriched and healthier baby food, improvements in weather forecasting, telemetry systems, a voice-controlled wheelchair, a programmable pacemaker—even a faster, more wind-resistant golf ball.

And all of these varied boons were made possible by bright, talented people, some of whom were standing on the shoulders of guys who built, flew, and trusted old World War II aircraft—and by a lot of others who are willing to support even a costly program that helps America stay out front.

### HUMAN RIGHTS

THE MOST BONE-CRUNCHING, spine-wrenching alterations in basic human conduct, however, came about at the uncompromising insistence of President Lyndon B. Johnson in the years 1964–66. Twisting arms, bending ears, maneuvering and manipulating, outthinking and outworking political opponents and stand-patters,

Johnson was determined to persuade America's most fortunate and most powerful to do our duty to help the most hapless and powerless among us.

This president's fixation was with the lot of the downtrodden, the dispossessed, and the discouraged, from whom fate had withheld any real participating share in the American dream. In particular, LBJ wanted our nation to do long-delayed justice to its racial minorities who'd been relegated by custom to the status of second-class citizens and forced to dwell in the shadows of our white majority.

The Supreme Court, in *Brown v. Board of Education* (1954), had ordered the public schools to integrate. But pervasive attitudes of unjust discrimination, so deeply ingrained in society by years of passivity, remained. The armed services had integrated racially, but throughout the South, the "best" stores, hotels, and restaurants systematically denied service to blacks. Even common public conveniences like city bus service, public water fountains, and restrooms discriminated.

And while three constitutional amendments a century earlier had formally conferred citizenship on former slaves and their progeny forever, in the real world a devil's brew of local contrivances—including poll taxes, voter "testing" subterfuges, and bald-faced intimidation—had kept millions of African-American citizens from voting.

There were some observers who saw Lyndon Johnson as a crude, devious, conniving politician, craftily calculating ways to enhance his own position in life. These people did not know the Lyndon Johnson I knew.

True, he could be as rough as sandpaper and testy as a barbed-wire fence; he could be equally as smooth as a baby's cheek—whatever the situation required. But, at heart, this compulsive overachiever wanted to help people, little people, those who'd never had a chance, those who needed his help and had nobody else to take up for them. That's what he did all his life.

Lyndon Johnson's commitment to civil rights was real. It went back to his childhood—to an intelligent, gentle mother who taught him to read before he was five. And to a father, Sam Ealy Johnson Jr., a member of the Texas Legislature at a time when jingoistic colleagues were trying to compound legal sanctions and solecisms against Johnson's German-descended neighbors in the Texas Hill County.

It goes back to his first job as a teacher, after doubling up and graduating in three years while working his way through Southwest Texas State Teachers College. Lyndon taught at Cotulla, Texas, where most of his students were Mexican-American children. It troubled him, he told me more than once, that these bright-eyed kids sometimes seemed to be lacking in spirit and energy because they were hungry, lacking in nutrition, and none of them had ever previously received any encouragement to believe they could someday see the inside of a university. Or hold a decent-paying job.

It was Johnson who, at the end of World War II, had interceded on behalf of a Mexican-American family whose son had been killed in battle, and his body denied interment at the local cemetery on racial grounds. Johnson arranged for the young man to be buried with military honors at Arlington National Cemetery.

In 1963—a hundred years after the Emancipation Proclamation—President John F. Kennedy asked Congress to pass a public accommodations bill. The bill would make it a federal offense for any establishment that holds itself out to the public as a purveyor of goods or services, to deny service to anyone on grounds of race, color, religion, or place of origin.

Kennedy was assassinated before that bill could be considered by Congress. I was with him on that fateful last trip to Texas, introduced him to an early morning crowd in Fort Worth, talked with him en route from Fort Worth to Dallas, rode in the motorcade and watched his body being carried into Parkland Hospital. It was the most traumatic day in my years of congressional service.

Following our sad return to Washington, Johnson—so recently sworn into office—scheduled a speech on Capitol Hill to tell Congress that he would spend the entire remainder of that term carrying out the unfinished agenda as set forth by his predecessor, John Kennedy. Part of that unfinished business was civil rights.

By the end of January, the public accommodations bill had cleared the House and Senate judiciary committees. It was handled supportively by a bipartisan pair, Committee Chairman Emanuel Celler, a Democrat from New York, and the ranking Republican, Bill McCulloch of Ohio.

Rubbing raw the skins of traditional southerners (people like seventy-two-year-old Bill Colmer of Mississippi and eighty-year-old Howard Smith of Virginia), the bill provoked prolonged debate that lasted for nine days, involving separate votes on more than one hundred amendments offered on the House floor. After almost sixty-seven hours of actual verbal debate, the 1964 bill passed the House by a vote of 290 to 130.

The spirit of World War II was invoked more than once by the bill's supporters, extolling the heroism of black Americans on the front lines of battle for our country. There were mentions of the 99th Fighter Squadron, composed exclusively of African-Americans, and references to the heroic Japanese Americans in the 442nd Regimental Combat Team.

The following year, Johnson now reelected in his own right, Congress pushed to passage the largest litany of major progressive (some would say "populist") legislation since the glory days of Franklin D. Roosevelt's New Deal. Some of the most consequential were the act creating Medicare, massive outlays improving access of financially improvident youth to universities, the "War on Poverty" bills, Food Stamps, an Open Housing law, Job Corps camps, and Clean Water and Clean Air expenditures. An astounding array of uplifting, opportunity-equalizing initiatives.

And there was the Voting Rights Act.

Following close on the heels of the imbroglio at Montgomery, Alabama, where local law enforcement officials used powerful fire hoses, bats, and police dogs to subdue and intimidate peaceful demonstrators whose primary appeal was for registering voters, a sense of moral outrage swept the nation. The president, riding the wave of public disgust, asked congressional leaders to schedule early action on a voting rights bill he promised to send to Congress on the week of March 15.

Then, on a Sunday evening, he called House Speaker John Mc-Cormack and asked to address a joint House-Senate session at 9 P.M. the following evening. Johnson made a powerful, emotional speech, citing ways in which African-American citizens had been systematically discouraged—and in numerous instances, literally prevented—from casting votes in national, state, and local elections.

Johnson decried "the long denial of equal rights to millions of Americans," insisting at the end that this was not a black or white problem, not a North or South problem, not a Democrat or Republican problem to be overcome, but an *American* problem. His closing words were: "And we shall overcome!" A Gallup poll taken during the days just following the speech showed the highest favorability rating of LBJ's whole White House career.

THAT REFORM, LIKE OTHERS of that era, passed easily, speeded by the tailwinds of public support. Each of these was fed, directly and indirectly, by spirits unleashed in the minds of those who'd returned from World War II. These few monuments I've mentioned are mostly composite symbols of multiple thousands of individual awakenings from dreams that cried out to come true.

This, then, is a message from many of us who went to war: Our country is transformed and its dreams fulfilled only as individual lives of our people can be transformed and fulfilled.

One identifying characteristic of Americans is that we are always trying to improve things. Walter Lippman wrote upon his retirement that he no longer believed human nature was perfectible, but he still believed it was improvable. It strikes me that the effort to improve it is part of what makes the process so enjoyable. And the ability to enjoy it is part of what makes that struggle so wonderfully worthwhile.

# ACKNOWLEDGMENTS

I HAVE MEANT THIS TO be an honest book, and have tried to write it so—to tell you just how things were. All the episodes of which I've written did occur, and I've done my best to tell them to you with fidelity. If I am wholly honest with you, though, I'll have to say that this is how it all *seemed to me*. There probably is no such thing as complete objectivity. Nobody records events with the cold, mechanical detachment of a camera. Everyone sees and remembers things through the prism of his or her own personal history and often unconsciously subjective reaction.

After six decades, it is hard to be absolutely certain that everything was *exactly* as I remember it to have been. Memory can play tricks on us. This is particularly true, I've found, regarding the precise sequence of events. It is possible that some things I remember as happening in a certain order, one following the other, actually occurred in reverse timing. I've stipulated actual dates only when I was sure of them.

But any such errors, to the extent they may exist, are not important to what I've tried to share with you, which is the underlying truth of things that were happening in that magical time and place, when all the world felt the war's impact and took its outcome very personally.

To help me keep things as factually straight as possible, I've had a lot of valuable assistance. Norma Ritchson, my research aide at Texas Christian University, has checked and rechecked details. Betty Hay Wright, my wife of the past thirty-two years, has read every chapter, critiquing it for readability.

Other veterans of the 380th have helped me to remember interesting aspects that had grown dim in my mind. Members of our Flying Circus group, over all these years, have observed an annual reunion. Sixty or more of us still try to get together somewhere every fall. I've drawn upon some of their records and individual recollections, as well.

Among my most trustworthy tools has been a series of scholarly publications, painstakingly researched and meticulously assembled, relating to the history of our 380th Bomb Group. Two of these volumes, entitled *We Went to War*, preserve a complete roster of every crew and each of its members, with details of their service. These were assembled and edited by Theodore J. Williams of West Lafayette, Indiana.

Another publication, on which I have relied heavily for factual accuracy (as well as inspiration), is a marvelous 510-page bound history of the group, *The Best in the Southwest*, by Glenn R. Horton Jr. Complete with many pictures gleaned from individual collections, it chronicles—by date, and in sequential order—the principal missions of the four squadrons, covering the entire life of the 380th from its inception in November 1942, to the war's end, in August 1945.

Glenn Horton and his brother, Gary, are the sons of Glenn R. Horton, a 529th Squadron pilot. These two have devoted years of scholarly work as official historians of the 380th. Without their help, my book of memories and musings would have been a thinner and less reliable account.

In the telling of this story, I have knowingly included one episode out of chronological sequence. The account of Virgil Stevens's strafing attack on the airdrome at Noemfoor, presented in

Chapter 21, tells of an event that occurred in the spring of 1944, after the landings of which I wrote in the two concluding chapters. I am indebted to Big Steve and others on that flight for helping me round out exactly what happened that day, as well as to Horton's written account, for their useful perspectives on the event.

If the portrait I've painted seems too rosily tinted, its lines too clearly drawn between the fuzzy realms of right and wrong, or too indulgent of our American assumption of righteous cause, what I have written may indeed reflect an unconscious generational bias on my part.

Just realize that I'm a product of those years when we all, big and small, were on the same team, when media figures like Edward R. Murrow and Ernie Pyle and Norman Rockwell influenced our perceptions. Every Hollywood actor, artist, and popular songwriter I can recall seemed firmly convinced of the inerrant rightness of our mission. To us the triumph of our cause was a necessity.

Many others dared more, suffered more, and achieved much more than I did. To them, and to their memories, I am thankful and profoundly respectful.

—JIM WRIGHT
TEXAS CHRISTIAN UNIVERSITY